KEEPING YOUR COOL

KEEPING YOUR COOL

A TEEN'S SURVIVAL GUIDE

LOU PRIOLO

P&R

PUBLISHING

P.O. BOX 817 • PHILLIPSBURG • NEW JERSEY 08865-0817

Unless otherwise indicated, Scripture quotations are from the *NEW AMERICAN STANDARD BIBLE*®. ©Copyright The Lockman Foundation 1960, 1962, 1963, 1968, 1971, 1972, 1973, 1975, 1977. Used by permission.

Verses marked (ccnt) are taken from Jay E. Adams, *The Christian Counselor's New Testament* (Hackettstown, NJ: Timeless Texts, 1994).

Scripture quotations marked (esv) are from the ESV® Bible (*The Holy Bible, English Standard Version*®), copyright © 2001 by Crossway. 2011 Text Edition. Used by permission. All rights reserved.

Scripture quotations marked (kjv) are from the King James Version.

Scripture quotations marked (nkjv) are from The Holy Bible, New King James Version. Copyright © 1979, 1980, 1982, Thomas Nelson, Inc.

Scripture quotations marked (niv) are from the HOLY BIBLE, NEW INTERNATIONAL VERSION®. NIV®. Copyright © 1973, 1978, 1984 by International Bible Society. Used by permission of Zondervan Publishing House. All rights reserved.

Scripture quotations marked (gnt) are from the Good News Translation in Today's English Version—Second Edition Copyright © 1992 by American Bible Society. Used by Permission.

Italics within Scripture quotations indicate emphasis added.

ISBN: 978-1-62995-018-1 (pbk)
ISBN: 978-1-62995-019-8 (ePub)
ISBN: 978-1-62995-020-4 (Mobi)

For clarity, some of the citations from Puritan authors contained in this volume have been modified slightly (rephrased into modern English).

Eye image © istockphoto.com / olgach

Printed in the United States of America

CONTENTS

Acknowledgments   7

1. I'm Not Angry!   9
2. The Volcano and the Clam   19
3. Learning to Communicate   33
4. Maintaining Your Cool   53
5. How to Handle Rejection and Hurt   65
6. Provocative Parents   79
7. Journaling Your Anger   99
8. Getting to the Heart of Anger, Part 1   115
9. Getting to the Heart of Anger, Part 2   129
10. Undoing Disrespect   155
11. Managing Manipulation   165
12. The Appeal Process   181
13. How to Talk to Your Parents about Their Sin   191
14. What Does It Mean to Be a Teen?   201

Appendix A: How to Become a Christian   215
Appendix B: How to Respond to Reproof   219

CONTENTS

Appendix C: Parental Provocation Worksheet   229

Appendix D: Idolatrous "Loves" in the Bible   233

Appendix E: Common Ways in Which Teenagers Sin
against Their Parents   237

Appendix F: Parental Evaluation Form   243

Appendix G: Extra Journals   247

ACKNOWLEDGMENTS

I DON'T REMEMBER their names. I was seated at a book table at a home educators' conference somewhere in Utah (or maybe it was Arizona) as two teenage sisters introduced themselves to me. They mentioned that they had read *The Heart of Anger* and enjoyed it.

"Enjoyed it?" I said. "Most people don't use the word *enjoy* when they describe how that book impacted them."

"Well, we did," they continued. "And we were wondering if you ever thought about writing a *Heart of Anger* for teens."

Their words struck me like lightning out of the blue. "No, I haven't. But that is a wonderful idea. I will seriously think and pray about doing that." It didn't take much of either for me to realize that such a book was needed.

I am very grateful to my two "little sisters" out there somewhere in "mountain-standard-time-zone land," who inspired me to do this project.

I would also like to acknowledge several others whose contributions have been invaluable:

The youth of Eastwood Presbyterian Church in Montgomery, Alabama, and their parents, who patiently sat through my "Getting to the Heart of Anger" Sunday school class (and asked lots of helpful "fine-tuning" questions about the material).

Alan and Linda McDaniel and Paul and Brenda Payne (and their families), who went through much of this material devotionally. (Linda and Brenda also made wonderful suggestions that made this book much more teen friendly than it otherwise would have been.)

ACKNOWLEDGMENTS

Anna Perry, who also proofread and helped to improve the readability of the book.

Melanie Clayton, who helped with chapter 9.

Fern Gregory, my incredible grammatical editor, who painstakingly read every word (probably two or three times) and who will mislead you into thinking that I really know how to write and spell properly.

And my wife, Kim, and my daughters, Sophia and Gabriella, who make lots of little sacrifices so that I can minister to others.

Thanks to everyone!

I'M NOT ANGRY!

"I CAN'T BELIEVE THIS! I'm sitting here reading a book that's over two hundred and fifty pages long about how to deal with my 'anger problem.' I didn't ask for this. Besides, I don't think I'm *that* angry. But I was given your book and told I had to read it. Thanks a lot, Lou Priolo! Who are you, anyway, and what gives you the right to tell me how to solve my so-called 'problem with anger'?"

I'm a counselor—a *biblical* counselor. This means that I depend not on psychology to help those who I counsel, but on God's Word. No, I really *don't* have any right to tell you how to solve your problems. It would be arrogant of me, a fellow sinner, to think that I did. Only God has the right to tell someone how to live his or her life. He does so in the Bible. One of the reasons the Bible was written is to show us how God wants us to behave (to think, to speak, and to act). It explains what kinds of attitudes and motives please Him and how, in dependence upon the Holy Spirit, we can correct the things in our lives that displease Him. So this book is about not so much what *I* think you ought to do to change, but what *the Bible* says about the things you can do to identify and correct sinful anger in your life.

"But I told you, I don't think I have that big a problem with anger."

Okay, that's fair. However, please give me a chance to show you how to deal with your anger issues even if they are relatively small. Sinful anger, in any form, can mess up our relationships. So what you learn as a result of reading this book will help you to improve your relationship not only with your parents and siblings, but also with your friends and, someday, with your spouse.

Besides, anger is something we all have to deal with each day of our lives; you are not alone in your struggle. You can find the word *anger* mentioned over *five hundred times* in the Bible (far more than the word *fear*, which appears over *three* hundred times). As a counselor, I have to help people deal with the sin of anger and its roots more than with any other sin. It's one of the most prevalent sins in all of life.

HOW DID I GET THIS WAY?

Unlike many psychological counseling theories that require years of analysis to determine exactly how each person got so messed up, the Bible teaches that we are all sinners. It tells us that we were born that way: "Surely I was sinful at birth, sinful from the time my mother conceived me" (Ps. 51:5 NIV; see also Eph. 2:3). Additionally, we can be influenced by others and can pick up (learn) other sinful habit patterns. "Do not be deceived: 'Bad company corrupts good morals' " (1 Cor. 15:33; see also 1 Cor. 5:6). Even our parents can influence us in wrong ways.

> Since you call on a Father who judges each man's work impartially, live your lives as strangers here in reverent fear. For you know that it was not with perishable things such as silver or gold that *you were redeemed from the empty way of life handed down to you from your fore-fathers*. (1 Peter 1:17–18 NIV)

According to Scripture, when an individual continually gives himself over to a particular sin, he eventually becomes bound by that sin (see John 8:34; Rom. 6:16; 2 Peter 2:19). At some point in this process, the effect of his sin begins to bleed over into other areas of his life (school, work, family, church, and health, for example). As his life becomes increasingly dominated by the characteristics and consequences of his sin (Gal. 6:7–8; James 1:8), the problem may become so severe that God classifies that person by the name of the sin that has mastered him.[1] One of the terms used to describe an individual who has given himself over to the sin of anger is "an angry man."

The Bible specifically warns us not to hang around this kind of person.

> Do not associate with a man given to anger;
> Or go with a hot-tempered man,
> Lest you learn his ways,
> And find a snare for yourself. (Prov. 22:24–25)

Come with me for a moment into my counseling office.

Jim and Linda[2] sat across the desk from me with tears in their eyes. They were frustrated because their son was so difficult to manage. Linda began their story:

"We can't control Joshua. He is determined to have his own way. We're embarrassed by how he talks to us. His teacher says he disrupts the whole class. She has even suggested that he may need to be placed on medication to control his behavior. I feel guilty and ashamed because I have failed as a mother. We don't know what to do, and I feel like there is no hope. We're so afraid that if Joshua doesn't get help now, he is going to be a first-class rebel in just a few years."

As Jim and Linda proceeded with their story, they were still wondering why the counseling center at which I work had a rather unusual policy regarding the counseling of kids. As a rule, unless a crisis or an emergency exists, I will not see a young person without first having two or three sessions with his parents. As I explained to Jim and Linda, the reason for this policy is not to allow them to gossip about or slander their son to me, nor is it that I might build a case against him. Rather, the purpose of this policy is to identify how Jim and Linda might be sinning

1. A person who continually gives himself over to the sin of drunkenness is classified by God as a *drunkard* (1 Cor. 6:10). One who continually gives himself over to folly is identified in Scripture as a *fool* (Prov. 26:11). So it goes for those who continually lie, steal, and fornicate. They shall be called *liars*, *thieves*, and *fornicators*. The complete list of characterological sins is too lengthy to cite here. Suffice it to say that "the evil deeds of a wicked man ensnare him; the cords of his sin hold him fast" (Prov. 5:22 NIV).

2. Jim and Linda are pseudonyms for a composite couple taken from actual counseling cases.

against Joshua so that I may help them to remove the beams from their own eyes before they attempt to remove the splinter from Joshua's.[3]

Jim and Linda continued providing me with information in answer to specific questions that I was asking to help me formulate a tentative diagnosis of the existing problems within their family. While this question and answer process continued, I listened for *patterns of behavior* that could be identified as "pathological" from a biblical point of view, "not in words taught us by human wisdom but in words taught by the Spirit, expressing spiritual truths in spiritual words" (1 Cor. 2:13 NIV).

After some time, I walked over to the white board in my office. I then began listing the patterns of behavior that they had described in Joshua. Based on his parents' observations, I identified eleven undesirable behavior patterns:

1. Outbursts of anger (temper tantrums)
2. Argumentation (quarrelsome debates)
3. Disrespect
4. Fighting (violence)
5. Animosity
6. Cruelty
7. Strife (antagonism)
8. Acts of vengeance
9. Malice
10. Bitterness
11. Discouragement (apathy and indifference)

"Can you see a common denominator in all these behaviors?" I asked.

"Yes! I never thought of it like that before," Linda said. "It's anger! Joshua has an anger problem."

3. There are 168 hours in every week. If I see Josh for one hour each week, only to send him back into an environment that is making it easier for him to sin and more difficult for him to overcome his sinful habits (rather than making it more difficult for him to sin and easier for him to overcome his sinful habits), my one hour of *good influence* may be neutralized by the many hours of *bad influence* to which he is being exposed in his own home.

Writing "anger" next to the list I had written, I explained, "It looks as though Joshua may have developed some of the characteristics of *the angry man* described in the book of Proverbs."

> An angry man stirs up strife,
> And a hot-tempered man abounds in transgression. (Prov. 29:22)

> Do not associate with a man given to anger;
> Or go with a hot-tempered man,
> Lest you learn his ways,
> And find a snare for yourself. (Prov. 22:24–25)

The question I would like you to be thinking about as you continue with this chapter is, Do I qualify as an angry person? That is, has anger so dominated my life that I could rightly be considered an honorary member of God's "angry person" club?" Perhaps your anger issues are not yet as severe as Joshua's, but any sin, if left unchecked, can and usually will lead to greater problems and consequences.

THE DEVELOPMENT OF REBELLION

Did you know that there is a connection between anger and rebellion? Anger often leads to rebellion against authority. This process develops not just in young people, but also in wives who rebel against their husbands, in employees who rebel against their employers, in church members who rebel against the authority of the church—and in anyone who sinfully rebels against a divinely appointed authority.

This anger-to-rebellion process often can be traced through five distinct steps. These five steps on the stairway to destruction are hurt, bitterness, anger, stubbornness, and finally rebellion.

Hurt (Wounded Spirit)

Proverbs 18:14 asks, "A wounded spirit who can bear?" (KJV). The first step in the process is a hurt that is spawned by an offense (real or perceived).[4] This hurt is the seed that often germinates and grows into a root of bitterness (Heb. 12:15). When someone does something to offend us, it's our mental and emotional response to the offense that produces the "hurt." Think about the last time someone hurt you. How did you respond? It's our sinful bent to defend (or protect) ourselves by reacting outwardly or inwardly with some form of anger.

Bitterness

Bitterness is the second step on the stairway. If you do not respond biblically to the hurt (this involves forgiving the sin, over-looking the sin, or realizing that the "offense" was not wrong in God's eyes), you may begin to rehearse the offense in your mind—reviewing it over and over again. The practice of continually reviewing and imputing (charging your offender with the fault or responsibility for) the offense violates 1 Corinthians 13:5 ("love doesn't keep records of wrongs" CCNT). It also cultivates the seed of hurt that matures into a "root of bitterness." And your "root of bitterness" may defile others in your life.[5] "See to it that no one comes short of the grace of God; that no root of bitterness springing up causes trouble, and by it many be defiled" (Heb. 12:15).

Anger

Anger is the third step on the stairway. This is the kind of anger to which the Bible warns fathers not to provoke their children (see Eph. 6:4; Col. 3:21). This sort of anger is not simply the momentary explosive type of fury that quickly dies down (the kind that typically follows *hurt* and precedes *bitterness*). Rather, it's the characterological (life-dominating) sort of anger of which I spoke earlier. It's the kind of anger that has

---

4. What your parents do to you may or may not be a sin. But, if they have not sinned against you, you ought not to be "offended." It's one thing to be disappointed when your parents do something that bugs you or disappoints you. But unless they sin in the process, technically they have committed no offense against you. If they have sinned, they are in need of repentance. If you are offended by something your folks do that is not a sin, *you* are in need of repentance. (You need to change your mind about being so "stressed" over something your parents did that doesn't offend God.)

5. Please notice that I said, "*may* defile," not "*will* defile." Christians may not knowingly allow themselves to be the "victims" of other men's sin.

become so habitual that it is now characteristic of one's personality. It's this "life-dominating anger" that the contents of this book have been especially designed to address.

Stubbornness (Insubordination)

This step immediately precedes full-blown rebellion. "Rebellion is as the sin of witchcraft, and stubbornness is as iniquity and idolatry" (1 Sam. 15:23 NKJV). The self-sufficient rebel in the making is guilty of idolatry because he believes that he has become the ruler of his own destiny. The picture of stubbornness here is that of a backsliding heifer *pushing* her front hooves into the ground to counteract her master who is trying to pull (or push) her forward. Look at it from your parents' perspective. Do you think they can relate to this picture?

Rebellion

A rebel is someone whose characteristics have gone beyond that of an *angry man* and have taken on the characteristics of the proverbial *fool*. There is no better and more comprehensive description in the Bible of a rebel than the same description given of the fool. In case you are wondering whether you have gone beyond the scope of an *angry man* to that of a *rebel*, I have a little test you can take. Read through the following list of characteristics of a fool and put a check next to the ones that describe you. Perhaps you can also find someone other than yourself (a parent, teacher, friend, or church leader) to evaluate you from another perspective.

25 CHARACTERISTICS OF A FOOL

Characteristics	Proverbs
☐ He despises wisdom and instruction	1:7
☐ He hates knowledge	1:22
☐ He hurts his mother	7:25
☐ He grieves his mother	10:1
☐ He enjoys devising mischief	10:23

☐ He is right in his own eyes   12:15

☐ He is quick to anger   12:16

☐ He hates to depart from evil   13:19

☐ He is deceitful   14:8

☐ He is arrogant and careless   14:16

☐ He rejects his father's instruction   15:5

☐ He despises his mother   15:20

☐ He does not respond well to discipline   17:10

☐ He does not understand wisdom   17:16

☐ He has a worldly focus (carnal value system)   17:24

☐ He grieves his father   17:25

☐ He does not consider discussing any viewpoint but his own   18:2

☐ He provokes others to strife and anger by the things he says   18:6

☐ He has a smart mouth that usually gets him into trouble   18:7

☐ He is quarrelsome (contentious)   20:3

☐ He is a spendthrift   21:20

☐ He repeats his folly (foolishness)   26:11

☐ He trusts in his own heart   28:26

☐ He cannot resolve conflicts   29:9

☐ He gives full vent to his anger   29:11

_____ Total Score (number of checked boxes)

How many of these characteristics are true of you? The higher your score, the more you will gain from reading this book. But even if you recognized only one or two "foolish characteristics" in your life, there is still much from which you can benefit in the pages ahead. Remember, the best insurance against the development of characterological rebellion is to prevent characterological anger: "Do not be eager in your heart to be angry, for anger resides in the bosom of fools" (Eccl. 7:9).

ANGER IN MY HEART

My first book, *The Heart of Anger*, was written to help parents of characterologically angry children to train them to deal with anger biblically. It teaches parents to help their children identify and correct both *external* and *internal* manifestations of sinful anger. This book will do the same for you. We will look first at learning how, by God's grace, you can control sinful, *external* manifestations of anger. Then (and more importantly), you will learn how to identify and correct the wrong kind of *internal* anger that resides in your heart.

However, if you do not have Christ in your heart (see Eph. 3:17), you will *not* be able to make those changes—at least not in a way that will please God. No one can make such changes apart from the Holy Spirit's enabling power. If you have any doubt that you are a true Christian, whose sins have been forever forgiven because of Christ's death on your behalf, and in whom the Holy Spirit dwells, let me urge you to not go on to chapter 2 until you have read appendix A, "How to Become a Christian."

2

THE VOLCANO AND THE CLAM

WHEN WE ARE FACED WITH any problem, the possibility exists for us to become angry. There are two extreme expressions of sinful anger to which people often resort. On one end of the spectrum is *internalization:* some people "clam up" when they get angry. These individuals withdraw, cry, pout, sulk, walk away, retreat to another room, go for a walk or a drive (without first committing to resolve the conflict later), and give those whom they believe caused the problem a "cold shoulder."

At the other end of the spectrum is *ventilation* ("A fool gives *full vent* to his anger," Prov. 29:11 NIV). Some people "blow up" when they get angry. These individuals resort to raising their voices, calling others inappropriate names, using profanity, throwing, hitting, and kicking things, using biting sarcasm, and various other forms of vengeance. Some people blow up first and then clam up; others clam up until the internal pressure builds to overflowing, at which time they blow up.

How do you respond when you get angry?

▨ Blow up
☐ Clam up
▪ Blow up, then clam up
☐ Clam up, then blow up

In what *specific* ways have you preferred to express your anger?

BLOW UP RESPONSES

- ☐ Yelling/screaming
- ☐ Throwing/kicking/hitting
- ☒ Talking back (quarreling)
- ☐ Using biting sarcasm
- ☐ Name-calling
- ☐ Using profanity
- ☐ Contemptuous speech

List the other forms of hateful or vindictive actions you prefer:

I leave the room ✓

I don't talk to them 4

a while ✓

CLAM UP RESPONSES

- ☐ Sulking
- ☐ Pouting
- ☐ Crying
- ☐ Withdrawing
- ☐ Retreating
- ☐ Going for a walk or a drive
- ☒ Giving the "cold shoulder"

List the other forms of hateful or vindictive actions you prefer:

BREAKING THE CIRCUIT

Think of the circuit breaker in your home. When you and your parents are communicating without anger, the circuits are open and the electricity is flowing. When one of you "blows up," it shuts the circuits, and the power is cut off. It has the same effect when one of you clams up. It's as if someone secretly breaks into the circuit breaker and silently throws the switch, interrupting the flow of current. How often does anger short-circuit the communication between you and your folks?

When my wife and I are having a conflict, we try to express our differing opinions to each other in the hope that one of us will persuade the other of his or her point of view. So we banter back and forth for five, ten, or twenty minutes until I persuade her, or she persuades me, or we meet somewhere in the middle (or we both conclude that it's perfectly fine for us to agree to disagree). If we were to diagram one of our arguments, it might look something like this:

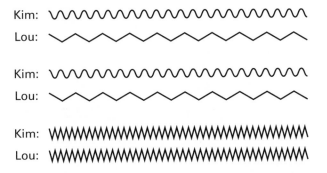

Back and forth we go, trying with each exchange of words to reach an agreement with each other with a minimal amount of sin (unbiblical communication). But the moment one of us becomes sinfully angry, the conflict comes to a halt. The communication circuit is broken and no further progress is made. Typically, the angry person exits the conflict prematurely or his opponent exits the conflict in fear. The conflict is aborted in midstream without biblical resolution.

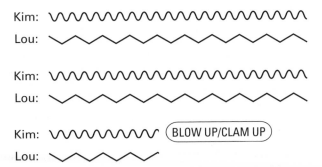

The expression of sinful anger is probably the greatest obstacle to resolving conflicts quickly. How is it with you? Think about your last conflict with your parents. Did it go south rather quickly after someone got angry? How about the last time you had a conflict with a sibling or a close friend? Chances are someone's anger stopped the two of you from resolving matters swiftly.

WHY DID GOD GIVE US ANGER?

At this point, I should probably explain that *not all anger is sinful.* There is such a thing as "righteous anger." God made each of us with the capacity to experience and enjoy a variety of emotions. Every emotion that God created has power for good as well as potential for evil.

"Every emotion? What about emotions like hate? Can it ever be good?"

Sure! In fact, as Christians, we are commanded to hate. "You who love the LORD, *hate* evil!" (Ps. 97:10 ESV). Listen to Solomon talk about hate in Proverbs 8:13: "The fear of the LORD is to hate evil; pride and arrogance and the evil way, and the perverted mouth, I hate."

God has placed in the human body the capacity to experience physical pain. He also put in the spirit of man the capability for painful emotions such as anxiety, fear, bitterness, loneliness, guilt, depression, rejection, despair, and, of course, anger. There is a positive function for these "negative" emotions.

Most of us would never seek the help of a physician unless we were in some kind of physical pain. Such pain, therefore, can be a good thing because it lets us know that something is wrong. Similarly, most people would never seek my help as a counselor unless they were in some kind of emotional distress. Our painful emotions can be good because they let us know that something is wrong in our lives.

Imagine lying in bed at 3:30 a.m. when all of a sudden the smoke detector in your house startles you from a sound sleep. You can't believe the audacity of that smoke detector—waking you up out of a sound sleep by piercing the night with its cacophonous 103-decibel distress signal! How are you ever going to get back to sleep with that continuous piercing alarm screaming in your ears?

"We'll just see about that!" you say to yourself as you jam your fingers into your ears, pull the pillow over your head, and try to fall back to sleep.

After ten more minutes of torment, you decide to unplug your ears and begin to grope around under your bed for the nearest shoe. Then you throw off the covers, jump out of bed, stomp off toward the smoke detector with boot in hand, and commence to smash the smoke detector to smithereens.

"That's absurd!"

Why is that absurd?

"Because the real problem is not with the smoke detector—it's with the fire that set off the smoke detector!"

Exactly! It's foolish to smash the smoke detector when it's doing what it was designed to do and is working only too well. Yet this is often the way people try to deal with their emotions. They ignore them, hoping the pain will go away. Or they turn to alcohol or drugs, or do whatever it takes to make the pain go away. In their desperation, they never stop to consider that the real problem may not be with their emotions at all, but with some other fire in their lives.

"Are you saying that all my distressing emotions are the result of my own sin?"

Certainly not. All misery, including most pain, is the result of sin, but not all pain is the result of *our own* sin. Christ was without sin, yet He was "a man of sorrows, and acquainted with grief" (Isa. 53:3; see also Matt. 26:38). He said, "Blessed are those who mourn" (Matt. 5:4). He could "sympathize with our weaknesses" (Heb. 4:15). He became angry (Mark 3:5) and indignant (Mark 10:14).[1] He wept over the death of His friend (John 11:34–35) and over the city of Jerusalem (Luke 19:41).

So not all potentially distressing emotions are the result of personal sin. They may simply be the normal result of adjusting to new and stressful circumstances that God has brought into our lives. They may be attributed to physiological causes, such as illness or fatigue.

---

1. In his gospel, Mark uses at least four different Greek words to describe the Lord's anger.

Since Jesus Christ was perfect and could not sin, He never experienced any emotion that was the result of His own sin. He never needed an emotional smoke detector to alert Him to personal wrongdoing. You and I, however, often experience feelings that warn us about sin in our lives.

Someone has said that anger is an emotion that God gives to us for the purpose of destroying something. If we "clam up" when we are angry, whom are we destroying?

"Ourselves?"

Right. We certainly do hurt the other person, but we end up hurting ourselves in the process.

And if we blow up, whom are we destroying with our anger?

"The person at whom we blow up!"

Exactly!

What do you suppose God wants you to destroy (or attack) with this anger? (Hint: look back at the beginning of this chapter.)

"The problem!"

Right again! God expects us to release our anger, under His control, toward *the problem*.

"OK; so how *exactly* do we do that?"

Since most of our "problems" have to do with people (have you ever noticed that when we get angry, it usually involves another person?), one thing is always necessary. What is it that we usually have to do in order to focus the anger from our hearts onto the problem (which usually involves someone else)? In other words, how do we direct the anger that is in our hearts to the other person without attacking him?

"I guess we have to talk to him."

Brilliant! Communication is necessary in order to get the problem solved. That means that if you are going to solve your issues with anger, you will have to learn how to communicate. In fact, I don't believe you will ever learn how to deal with your anger properly without making it your goal to become proficient in biblical communication. I'll have much more to say about that later. For now, let's see what the situation looks like when we factor in the communication element.

It's sort of like the game of darts. God has given us a set of darts that were designed for good purposes. When you get angry, the adrenal glands in your body pump out adrenaline, which enables you to take action. The action that you take will have consequences. If you choose to respond by fighting (blowing up) or by taking flight (clamming up), the problem will not be solved. More importantly, God will not be pleased with your efforts. Are you going to throw the dart at your opponent in a sinful sort of way? Are you going to swallow the dart and hurt yourself in an equally sinful sort of way?[2] Or are you going to learn how to throw the dart at the problem so as not to injure the other person by your words, attitudes, and actions?

Think about this. When you blow up, you are *mis*communicating. When you clam up, you are *not* communicating. Either way, you are not doing with the dart what God intended for you to do.

"But it's my parents! They are the ones who are causing the problem." Perhaps, but you still must learn how to talk to them if you want to deal with the problem God's way. When you don't, you add an entirely new problem to the mix by pushing their buttons (provoking them to anger). At that point, your folks, if they are like most parents I know, will probably have a very difficult time concentrating on what you are trying to tell them (regardless of how convincing your arguments are). At that moment, they will be more concerned with this angry, disrespectful teenager whom they "have tried to raise properly for the last umpteen years with apparently very little success." You shoot yourself in the foot when you resort to using sinful anger with your parents.

There is something else about anger and communication that I want you to know before I conclude this chapter. Your communication involves more than just words. When you are angry, your anger is communicated in three distinct ways.

---

2. Many people seem to think that clamming up is a much better "anger response" than blowing up—especially in light of Scripture passages that admonish Christians to keep quiet (see Proverbs 10:19; 17:27-28; James 1:19). Consequently, they do not see clamming up as a sin. But it often is. When God tells us, for example, that we should confront our habitually sinning brother (Matt. 18:15; Luke 17:3) or speak to protect someone from danger (Ps. 82:4; Prov. 24:11), we sin if we do not speak. Additionally, these clam-up responses are often motivated by vengeance, which the Bible expressly forbids us to take for ourselves (Rom. 12:17-21).

THREE ELEMENTS OF COMMUNICATION

Communication involves more than just words (see Prov. 16:24). It also involves our tone of voice (see Prov. 16:21) and our nonverbal communication (see Acts 12:17). If you are going to learn how to communicate properly, you must learn how to do so in all three areas.

Of the three slices of this "communication pie," the Bible places the greatest emphasis on *words*.

With words, people can be motivated, encouraged, pierced, or healed.

With words, conflicts can be resolved and people's problems can be solved.

With words, precise meaning is communicated.

With words, God reveals Himself to man.

With words, we communicate the gospel to others.

With words, our minds comprehend the truth of God.

With the words of Scripture, when internalized by the Christian, the Holy Spirit somehow transforms our lives into the image of Christ.

With words, the man of God brings doctrine, reproof, correction, and instruction in righteousness.

With words, man will be justified.

With words, man will be condemned.

If there is ever a time when a believer ought to premeditate what he is going to say, it's in those circumstances when he is most likely to become angry. When we are angry (or experiencing other intense emotions), we are at greatest risk of sinning with our words. Controlling our anger means choosing our words carefully, especially when a problem exists that makes us angry.

The heart of the righteous studies how to answer. (Prov. 15:28 NKJV)

The heart of the wise teaches his mouth,
And adds learning to his lips. (Prov. 16:23 NKJV)

Your words, even the careless ones, will be examined on the day of judgment. They will justify you or condemn you.

And I say to you, that every careless *word* that men shall speak, they shall render account for it in the day of judgment. For by your *words* you shall be justified, and by your *words* you shall be condemned. (Matt. 12:36–37)

Other people also judge us by our words. Your parents make judgments about you based on what they hear you say. Do your words justify you in their minds, or do they condemn you?

With your words, you can harm them or heal them. "There is one who speaks rashly like the thrusts of a sword, but the tongue of the wise brings healing" (Prov. 12:18). You can build them up or tear them down. "Let no unwholesome word proceed from your mouth, but only such a word as is good for edification according to the need of the moment, that it may give grace to those who hear" (Eph. 4:29). Your words can encourage them or discourage them (see Deut. 1:28; 1 Thess. 4:18; 5:11; Heb. 3:13).

USE THE APPROPRIATE TONE OF VOICE

The Bible also addresses the importance of using the proper tone of voice. "A gentle answer turns away wrath, but a harsh word stirs up anger" (Prov. 15:1). "Sweetness of speech increases persuasiveness" (Prov. 16:21; see also Judg. 1:8; Prov. 16:24; 18:23; Col. 4:6). It's not enough for us to choose the right words. We must say the right words in a tone that is appropriate.

Teenagers probably provoke their parents to anger more quickly by being disrespectful than by any other behavior. Yet it's more often the tone of the teen's voice, rather than the words, that communicates disrespect. In fact, some communication professionals believe that in the English language, the message is communicated up to seven times more by the tone of one's voice than by one's words.

For example, suppose your mom were to ask you, "Honey, would you like some more meatloaf?" Your "No, thank you" could be interpreted in two very different ways depending on your tone of voice.

"No [I couldn't eat another bite], thank you [because that was so good, I've already had three helpings]," you say with a pleasant inflection in your voice.

Or you gruffly bark out, "No, thank you [I almost gagged forcing myself to swallow this slop]!"

Think about the many bad attitudes your voice inflection is capable of communicating. There is disrespect, anger, hatred, bitterness, contempt, vengeance, fear, anxiety, pride, condescension, harshness, superiority, self-righteousness, sarcasm, criticism, callousness, impatience, and indifference, to name a few. On the other hand, with the tone of your voice you can also communicate such righteous attitudes as love, acceptance, compassion, forgiveness, patience, submissiveness, forbearance, humility, and gentleness.

USE THE APPROPRIATE FORMS OF NONVERBAL COMMUNICATION

The Bible has much to say about nonverbal forms of communication. Nonverbal communication encompasses such things as your facial expressions, eye contact, gestures, posture, and touch. Some believe that our body language carries even more of the total communication message than words and tone of voice put together.[3]

Perhaps the best place to begin is with your face. "Why are you angry?" the Lord asked Cain. "And why has your countenance fallen?" (Gen. 4:6). Anger is one of several sins that the Bible specifically indicates can show up on your face.[4] What is in your heart also bleeds through to your countenance (see Neh. 2:2; Prov. 15:13; Eccl. 7:3). In the Bible, the word *heart* represents the "inner man," and it's invariably held against the "outer man" (mouth, tongue, lips, eyes, countenance, hands, feet, etc.). Isaiah put it this way: "The expression of their faces bears witness against them. And they display their sin like Sodom" (Isa. 3:9).

David refers to God as "the help of my countenance" (Ps. 42:11; 43:5). He realized that only God could remove from one's heart the sins

3. This is probably not as it should be. Although the Bible addresses all three forms of communication, the sheer preponderance of references argues that our *words* should be given the most significant attention.

4. For information on a recording entitled "How to Improve Your Looks from the Inside," which further develops the subject of the specific sins that can mar our countenances, please visit http://www.loupriolo.com.

that mar the countenance. Solomon also understood the connection between man's heart (the reservoir of wisdom; see Prov. 2:10; 14:33; 17:16) and his face. "A man's wisdom illumines him and causes his stern face to beam" (Eccl. 8:1).

Did you know that pride, anger, bitterness, fear, sensuality, and rebellion can all show on our faces without our knowledge? That's right. There are at least eight attitudes that can mess up your face if they remain too long in your heart.

Pride

> The wicked, in the haughtiness of his countenance, does not seek Him.
> All his thoughts are, "There is no God." (Ps. 10:4)

Anger

> But for Cain and for his offering He had no regard. So Cain became very angry and his countenance fell. (Gen. 4:5)

Bitterness

> Now Jacob heard the words of Laban's sons, saying, "Jacob has taken away all that was our father's, and from what belonged to our father he has made all this wealth." And Jacob saw the attitude of Laban, and behold, it was not friendly toward him as formerly. (Gen. 31:1–2)

Fear

> Suddenly the fingers of a man's hand emerged and began writing opposite the lampstand on the plaster of the wall of the king's palace, and the king saw the back of the hand that did the writing. Then the king's face grew pale, and his thoughts alarmed him; and his hip joints went slack, and his knees began knocking together. (Dan. 5:5–6)

Sensuality

> Do not desire her beauty in your heart,
> Nor let her catch you with her eyelids. (Prov. 6:25)

Rebellion

> The eye that mocks a father,
> And scorns a mother,
> The ravens of the valley will pick it out,
> And the young eagles will eat it. (Prov. 30:17)

Guilt

> And I said, "O my God, I am ashamed and embarrassed to lift up my face to Thee, my God, for our iniquities have risen above our heads, and our guilt has grown even to the heavens. "Since the days of our fathers to this day we have been in great guilt, and on account of our iniquities we, our kings and our priests have been given into the hand of the kings of the lands, to the sword, to captivity, and to plunder and to open shame, as it is this day. (Ezra 9:6–7)

Selfishness

> Do not eat the bread of a selfish man [literally, "one who has an evil eye"],
> Or desire his delicacies. (Prov. 23:6)

Now, since you can neither hear nor see the look on your own face, detecting inappropriate facial expressions is much more difficult than detecting wrong words or voice inflections. You will need the assistance of others (your parents and perhaps your siblings and friends) to correct any inappropriate facial casts. Have you ever asked them to let you know when your face is saying something wrong? (I know; your parents do it quite regularly without your having to ask.)

The single best correction you can make is to smile. One smile can often "cover a multitude of sins." At the very least, smiling lets people know that you are *trying* to communicate in a warm, friendly, pleasant, kind, and proactive sort of way. As we will see later, the long-term solution to improving your looks is to do it from the inside out by cooperating with the Spirit of God as He develops in you the character of the Lord Jesus Christ.

In some cultures of the world, it's considered rude to look people in the eyes. In our culture, it's generally considered rude not to look at people when talking to them. The Bible says in 1 Corinthians 13:5 that love "is not rude" (NIV). When God counsels us, He is said to do so with His eye upon us (Ps. 32:8). Job said to one of his counselors, "And now please look at me, and see if I lie to your face" (Job 6:28). One of the clues that may indicate a potential lie (or at least some kind of fearful emotion) is the dilation of the speaker's eyes. Look at your parents when they are talking to you. As much as possible, make it a habit to practice "Stop, look, and listen" when they are addressing you. *Stop* what you're doing when they begin talking to you (e.g., put down the iPhone or the magazine, turn off the television set), *look* directly at their eyes, and *listen* intently to what they are saying to you.

A final element of nonverbal communication we should consider addressing is touch. The importance of expressing physical affection can be seen in the life of Jesus. John, the disciple "whom Jesus loved," "was reclining on Jesus' breast" (John 13:23). Jesus showed His compassion for quite a few people as He touched them in the process of healing their infirmities. In the context of marriage and the family, certain forms of touching (affection) are used to communicate feelings such as love, compassion, comfort, and sympathy. How affectionate are you to your parents?

In the next chapter, we will continue to look at the importance of communication, especially as it relates to anger-producing problems.

3

LEARNING TO COMMUNICATE

HARVEY AND PRISCILLA, a married couple, were seated facing each other in my counseling office, attempting to resolve a conflict. Soon after they began speaking, Priscilla made a very nasty, sarcastic, and spiteful comment to Harvey.

"Whoa!" I said. "Priscilla, those words were not honoring to your husband. Would you please try saying that again?"

At that point, I took the essence of what she was apparently trying to say to Harvey and reworded it in a much more gracious fashion than her original version.

"Try it this way," I said, attempting to put into her mouth (verbatim) an amended version of her thoughts.

I'll never forget what happened next. Looking Harvey straight in the eyes, she opened her mouth, but nothing came out. She just sat there with her mouth open and her tongue sort of dangling in midair between her upper and lower sets of teeth.

"Go on. You can do it," I said encouragingly.

After momentarily closing her mouth (for a rest), she tried it again. When she did, a rather raspy, hissing, guttural, choking kind of sound came out, but nothing else.

"It's really hard for me to say those words," she said to me with an inquisitive look on her face.

After reflecting momentarily, I asked, "Would you like to know why?"

"Tell me, please!"

"What I asked you to say to Harvey was quite gracious and humble. The reason you are so speechless, Priscilla, is because there is not enough grace and humility in your heart to utter those words without choking on them."

She finally understood that she could not truly sweeten her speech without first changing her heart.

The Bible speaks often of the connection between the heart and the mouth (and lips and tongue).[1] Two verses in Proverbs 15 use the words *spout* (v. 2) and *pour* (v. 28) to describe the tongue and the mouth respectively. The picture that comes to mind is that of a pitcher.

> The *tongue* of the wise makes knowledge acceptable,
> But the mouth of fools *spouts* folly. (Prov. 15:2)

> The heart of the righteous ponders how to answer,
> But the mouth of the wicked *pours out evil things.* (Prov. 15:28)

In this analogy, the inside or *reservoir* of the pitcher (which holds the liquid) corresponds to your heart. The *spout* of the pitcher corresponds to your mouth (or lips or tongue). Whatever is in the reservoir will "pour out" of the spout when the pitcher is appropriately tilted. If the reservoir contains milk, milk will pour out of the spout. If it contains coffee, coffee will pour out. If gasoline is put in, then gasoline will flow out. And so it is with whatever fluid (whether palatable or poisonous) is contained in the pitcher. It's just as Jesus said: "The mouth speaks out of that which fills the heart. The good man out of his good treasure brings forth what is good; and the evil man out of his evil treasure brings forth what is evil" (Matt. 12:34–35).

You can't expect to speak that which is good if there is evil in your heart. Jesus asked the question, "How can you, being evil, speak what is good?" (Matt. 12:34). The only way to have your heart truly cleansed

1. See 1 Samuel 1:13; Job 33:3; Psalm 12:2; 17:10; 19:14; Proverbs 15:2, 28; 16:23; 26:23–24; Matthew 15:8.

is through the regenerating work of the Holy Spirit,[2] who indwells only those who have put their faith in the Lord Jesus Christ. This must be followed by His sanctifying work.[3] (For a more thorough explanation of what it is to be a genuine Christian, please take a moment to read appendix A, "How to Become a Christian," if you have not yet done so.) What you will learn as a result of reading this chapter can help you to be a better communicator. But if you are not a Christian, and if you are not willing to allow God to clean up the junk that is in your heart, all the hi-tech, state-of-the-art biblical communication principles you will learn will do you little good. It will be like trying to erect a skyscraper on a foundation made of sand and clay.

COMMUNICATION IS OUR BUSINESS

Have you ever had a seemingly obscure conversation with someone, only to walk away from it and realize you learned something profound? Let me tell you about something I learned a few years ago. The music minister at the church I was attending engaged me in a discussion (actually it was more like a lecture) about why the church needed a new public address system. I never understood why he was trying to persuade me, since I had no authority and little ability to help him. Nevertheless, during the course of his pitch he said something that made a profound impact on my life.

His exact words were, "If we Christians are in any business at all, it's the communication business." As he spoke those words, I knew that he was right. When the conversation was over, I couldn't get this thought out of my mind. The more I pondered it and studied my Bible, the more I realized how true his expression was. As I meditated on some of the many passages of Scripture supporting his statement, I was amazed to discover how many ways we Christians are instructed to use communication effectively.

2. *Regeneration* is a work of the Holy Spirit whereby He enters the lives of those who were spiritually dead and quickens them—makes them spiritually alive, enabling them to live a new (kind of) life by His transforming power.

3. *Sanctification* is a work of the Holy Spirit whereby He progressively transforms regenerated individuals into the image of Christ—enabling them to grow in holiness.

Consider, for instance, the great commission: "Go into all the world and *preach* the gospel to every creature" (Mark 16:15 NKJV). *Preach* is a communication word. Or consider Matthew 28:19–20: "Go therefore and make disciples of all the nations, baptizing them in the name of the Father and the Son and the Holy Spirit, *teaching* them to observe all that I commanded you." Teaching is a form of communication that is essential in making disciples. Then there is Ephesians 4:15: "But *speaking* the truth in love, we are to grow up in all aspects into Him, who is the head, even Christ." When the *truth* is communicated in love, it enables the believer to grow and mature in Christ.

Solomon wrote many proverbs about communication. Perhaps his most comprehensive verse is found in Proverbs 18:21: "Death and life are in the power of the tongue." The power of your words is tremendous. They are far more potent than you probably realize. With your tongue you can kill or you can heal.[4] You can save or you can destroy. Solomon continues in the second line of that same verse, "And those who love it will eat its fruit." That is, if you make use of (love) the power of the tongue, you will see its results (eat its fruit). If you use your tongue for your own selfish purposes, you will end up hurting people. If, on the other hand, you use your tongue to build people up, you can influence them greatly, and you will experience tremendous satisfaction ("With the fruit of a man's mouth his stomach will be satisfied; he will be satisfied with the product of his lips," Prov. 18:20).

Take my job for example. As a biblical counselor, I have the joy of regularly seeing people's lives transformed. People are changed in very significant ways as a result of this special kind of counseling that I do. Of course, I'm not the one who changes them—God's Spirit does that. There is, however, something I do from the human perspective to facilitate these changes. What is it? I ask questions, I listen, and I talk. I *communicate*. I explain to people what the Bible has to say about their problems. I use the Scriptures to teach, to convict, to correct, and to instruct in righteousness (see 2 Tim. 3:16), and somehow the Spirit of

---

4. See Proverbs 12:18: "There is one who speaks rashly like the thrusts of a sword, but the tongue of the wise brings healing."

God uses His Word to change lives, transforming them and conforming them to the image of Christ. Teaching, convicting, correcting, and instructing in righteousness all involve communication. Yes, words are powerful—especially God's words spoken by His ministers for His purposes.

It's true! If you are in any business at all, Christian teenager, you are in the communication business.

PREREQUISITE TO ANY RELATIONSHIP

Have you ever stopped to consider that if it were not for the Bible (God's revelation of Himself to man), you would not know enough about Him to be saved, let alone to have an intimate relationship with Him? You might know through general revelation[5] that God exists, but it takes special revelation[6] (the Bible) for you to know how to be saved, how to glorify Him, and how to enjoy fellowship with Him. To the extent that God reveals Himself to you, you may have a relationship with Him. To the extent that you do not comprehend His revelation, your intimacy with Him will be adversely affected. *Revelation is a prerequisite to having a relationship.*

The same principle holds true in all relationships (see John 15:15). To the degree that two people reveal themselves to one another, they will experience relational intimacy. Someday, you will likely marry. Since marriage (becoming one flesh) is the most intimate (closest) of personal relationships, the revelation of yourself to your future spouse will exceed the revelation of yourself to any other person (except the Lord, who knows you more intimately than you know yourself; see Ps. 139:1–6).

We read in Genesis 2:24–25,

5. *General revelation* is that which may be generally known about God (such as His eternal power and Godhead; see Rom. 1:20) through His creation.

6. *Special revelation* (the Bible) is necessary because of the limitations of general revelation to fallen man. General revelation is incapable of describing the many perfections of God, which are necessary to glorify and enjoy Him. Also, man's sinfulness distorts his ability to perceive God through natural revelation. Additionally, God's transcendency (the fact that He is far above our ability to fully comprehend) makes it impossible for man to understand Him apart from special revelation.

For this cause a man shall leave his father and his mother, and shall cleave to his wife; and they shall become *one flesh*. And the man and his wife were both *naked* and were *not ashamed*.

Adam and Eve's "nakedness" speaks not only of their lack of clothing, but mostly of the total openness and frankness that they enjoyed with each other before they sinned. It's our sin (especially the sin of pride) that keeps us from being as candid and straightforward as Adam and Eve were before the fall. It is God's intention for Christian husbands and wives to increasingly become more and more "naked and unashamed" with each other, as were our forefathers in the garden.

"But I'm not married now; I'm only a teenager."

Of course you are. But are you practicing?

"Practicing?"

That's right. Someday you will have to learn how to open up to that special someone like you never have before. You'll have to "pull back the curtain" (that's really what revelation means) of your heart and let another person see what's inside. If you are not in the habit of pulling back the curtain with your parents (for example), who have a biblical need to know certain things that are going through your mind, how do you think you will do with your spouse?

COMMON HINDRANCES TO REVELATION

If you have any hope of learning how to manage your anger, you have to learn how to communicate according to biblical principles. In this next section, we are going to look at some of the sinful forms of communication that in one way or another contribute to anger—the anger in your own heart or the anger that you provoke in others by your miscommunication. Although these abuses of speech affect all your relationships, I will center our thoughts on how they may impact your relationship with your parents. If there is anyone else in your life with whom you have difficulties communicating, you may want to reread this section, inserting the names of those individuals in the appropriate places.

Interruption

Few things kill the free-flowing exchange of ideas like interruption. Whether it's in the middle of a sentence or of a dialogue, when you interrupt your parents before they finish their thoughts, you violate several scriptural principles. To begin with, you show yourself to be quick to speak and slow to hear. This is the very opposite of what God commands: "But let everyone be quick to hear, slow to speak and slow to anger" (James 1:19). Second, you err by beginning your argument (or point of view) before you have heard out your parents. The Bible says, "He who gives an answer before he hears, it is folly and shame to him" (Prov. 18:13). This is especially provocative to parents. Not only is it inconsiderate, but it also communicates a "know it all" attitude that essentially says, "I know where you're going with that, and you're wrong. Let me tell you how it really is." Let your folks finish their arguments before you end up playing the fool and tempting them to focus on your character rather than on your "case."

Inattentiveness

"May I go to the movies?" Melanie asks her father with her headphones snugly in place. While her father attempts to answer, Melanie is distracted by one of her favorite songs, which just that moment began playing on her new iPod. So she continues to listen to the music, singing along in her heart, all the while pretending to be attentive. She smiles, looks her father straight in the eyes, and nods politely as he continues to wax eloquently. But her mind is light-years away.

It's especially irksome to parents when their children do not pay attention to them. Perhaps this is because it's a form of rudeness. Perhaps because the impertinent attitude communicated by inattentiveness says, in effect, "What you have to say doesn't concern me. It isn't really important (and, by the way, neither are you)."

Another version of inattentiveness occurs when a teenager hears the first part of what his or her parents are saying but quickly "tunes them out" in the process of mentally formulating a response. "A fool finds no pleasure in understanding but delights in airing his own opinions" (Prov. 18:2 NIV). Like Elihu (Job's wise friend), who paid close attention (Job 32:11; 33:1, 33) to Job and his other counselors (who themselves answered a matter before they heard it and were reproved for their folly and shame), you should pay close attention to what your parents are saying to you. The book of Proverbs uses a variety of terms to describe a child's responsibility to be attentive to his parent. Here are a few of them (to which I have added italics to emphasize my point). Notice that the idea behind these verses is not just to be attentive to your parents' instruction, but to be so attentive that you commit the instruction to memory. Think about that the next time you have to tell your folks that you forgot what they told you to do.

> *Hear*, my son, your father's instruction,
> And *do not forsake* your mother's teaching. (Prov. 1:8)

> *Hear*, O sons, the instruction of a father,
> And *give attention* that you may gain understanding,
> For I give you sound teaching;
> *Do not abandon* my instruction. (Prov. 4:1–2)

> My son, *give attention* to my words;
> *Incline your ear* to my sayings.
> *Do not let them depart* from your sight;
> *Keep them* in the midst of your heart. (Prov. 4:20–21)

> My son, *give attention* to my wisdom,
> *Incline* your ear to my understanding. (Prov. 5:1)

> My son, observe the commandment of your father,
> And do not forsake the teaching of your mother;
> Bind them continually on your heart;
> Tie them around your neck.
> When you walk about, they will guide you;
> When you sleep, they will watch over you;
> And when you awake, they will talk to you. (Prov. 6:20–22)

My son, keep my words,
And treasure my commandments within you.
Keep my commandments and live,
And my teaching as the apple of your eye.
Bind them on your fingers;
Write them on the tablet of your heart. (Prov. 7:1–3)

Now therefore, my sons, listen to me,
And pay attention to the words of my mouth. (Prov. 7:24)

Judging Motives

What's wrong with the following statements?

"You only said that because you want me to feel guilty."

"The reason you're being nice to me is so I won't embarrass you in front of your friends."

"You don't want me to have any fun."

"You only want to be a biblical parent so that you can impress your friends at church."

The problem with each of these judgments is that it presupposes an evil motive. Unless your folks specifically tell you exactly what their motives are (what they want or why they do what they do, etc.), you may not take it upon yourself to presume (or deduce) to know them. You may rightfully evaluate their words and actions (and perhaps their attitudes), but you may not judge the motives of another. (You may not, as a judge, slam the gavel down in your mind or with your mouth and pronounce someone guilty of having evil motives.) "Therefore do not go on passing judgment before the time, but wait until the Lord comes who will both bring to light the things hidden in the darkness and disclose the motives of men's hearts; and then each man's praise will come to him from God" (1 Cor. 4:5).

Now, if you have a suspicion about your parents' motives, there *may* be a time and a place to ask them to judge their motives for themselves and *perhaps* tell you what they are (e.g., "Mom, I was wondering what motivated you to say that. Would you mind helping me

41

understand?" See Eccl. 3:7).[7] The key biblical principle behind this issue is 1 Corinthians 13:7: "[Love] believes all things" (it believes the best). Love, in the absence of real evidence, puts the best possible interpretation on the facts. Is that what you do in your heart with your parents? Is that what you do with your siblings? Is it what you do with your friends?

Blame Shifting

This is literally the oldest trick in "The Book." "The woman whom you gave to be with me, she gave me fruit of the tree, and I ate" (Gen. 3:12 ESV). Pride not only blinds us to our own sin, it also looks for someone other than ourselves to blame. You must "first take the log out of your own eye, and then you will see clearly to take the speck out of your brother's [or parent's] eye" (Matt. 7:5). When your parents reprove you, don't immediately look for a way out of trouble by looking for someone else to blame. Rather, be willing to assume 100 percent of the responsibility for your own sin (even if you believe you are only 5 percent wrong and your parents are 95 percent wrong).

Apologizing (Rather Than Asking for Forgiveness)

"Why do you say that apologizing is not biblical?"

I say it because saying "I'm sorry" does not thoroughly deal with the offense.

You say, "Mom, I'm sorry for not cleaning up my room as you had told me to do."

She says, "You sure are sorry! You're one of the sorriest kids I've ever met!"

The ball is still up in the air when you simply say, "I'm sorry." The loose ends are not tied up biblically. You both may walk away not knowing whether the issue is resolved (i.e., never to be brought up again). By asking the one against whom you have sinned to forgive you, you secure certain commitments from her that will truly put the offense behind you both and will tie up any loose ends.

---

7. If your parents have just asked you to do something, *obey them first* before attempting to find out what they are thinking.

Sweeping Generalizations

What is invariably wrong about making statements such as these to your parents?

"You *never* listen to me."

"You're *always* dissatisfied with *everything* I do."

"The *only* time you're nice to me is when you want me to do something for you."

"You are the *worst* mother I've ever known."

In addition to being disrespectful and unloving, these statements are dishonest. They are lies! "Laying aside falsehood," the Bible says, "speak truth, each one of you, with his neighbor, for we are members of one another" (Eph. 4:25). It's almost certainly not true that your parents (your closest neighbors) are *always* or *never* or *only* as bad as you make them out to be when you use such inaccurate language. Using such inaccurate terminology can lead to arguments over the frequency of the problem and can sidestep the real issue (e.g., "That's not true! I haven't embarrassed you in front of your friends for at least three weeks!").

Not Communicating Willingly

One of the most common communication difficulties I encounter in my counseling office is people who are passive rather than active in the communication process. That is, they sit passively by, expecting those with whom they are supposed to be conversing to take virtually all the initiative. Rather than volunteering all the data necessary for the dialogue, these inactive individuals expect their counterparts to drag out of them all but the most basic information. This seems to be more common in men than in women, so guys, I want you to pay especially close attention to this one. The reluctance to communicate is not in keeping with God's design for man to be the leader (and initiator) of the marital relationship. A husband simply does *not* have the right to not engage his wife in the communication that is so essential to a one-flesh relationship. There are many things that a husband has a biblical responsibility to discuss with his wife (e.g., problems that she perceives in the marriage relationship, her personal problems, a variety of issues

43

WHAT DOES IT MEAN TO FORGIVE?

You are commanded to forgive, "just as God in Christ also has forgiven you" (Eph. 4:32). What does that mean? God says, "I, even I, am the one who wipes out your transgressions for My own sake; and I will *not remember* your sins" (Isa. 43:25) and "I will forgive their iniquity, and their sin I will *remember no more*" (Jer. 31:34).

So does God have amnesia? Certainly not! God is omniscient (all knowing) and knew about your sins even before you committed them. When the Bible speaks of God forgetting our sins, it refers to the fact that when a person has truly been forgiven by God, He does not hold these sins against the forgiven sinner. He doesn't charge them to his account. Rather, God will charge them to the account of the Lord Jesus Christ, who died on the cross to pay the penalty of guilty sinners like you and me. Christ's death was a substitution. He died to take the punishment for our sin so that we, as saved individuals, might be credited with His righteousness. When we truly believe the gospel, God *promises* not to hold our sins against us. Instead He imputes the perfect righteousness of His Son to our account. What is the gospel (or "good news")? The gospel is simply this: if we repent and place our faith in what Christ has done by substituting Himself for us on the cross and rising from the dead, God promises to forgive all our sins and give us eternal life.

Forgiveness, therefore, is first and foremost a *promise*. As God promised not to hold the sins of repentant sinners against them, so we also must promise not to hold the sins of those we've forgiven against them. You may demonstrate this promise by *not* doing at least *three* things to the person you've forgiven. First, you may not bring up the forgiven offense to the forgiven person so as to use it against him or her. Second, you may not discuss the forgiven offense with others. Finally, you may not dwell on the forgiven offense yourself, but rather remind yourself that you have forgiven your offender "just as God in Christ also has forgiven you."*

---

* For a thorough treatment of biblical forgiveness, see Jay E. Adams, *From Forgiven to Forgiving: Learning to Forgive One Another God's Way* (Amityville, NY: Calvary Press, 1994).

When you ask for forgiveness (rather than simply apologizing), you secure for yourself those three promises. Isn't that much better than leaving the ball up in the air? Wouldn't you rather tie up those loose ends by having your parents commit to not holding your offense against you ever again? In light of this, I'd like to suggest a very effective approach that a teenager can use when seeking forgiveness from an offended parent.

First: Acknowledge that you have sinned. Let your mother or father know that you realize what you did was wrong.

Example: "I was wrong for not obeying you when you asked me twice to clean up my room before I went out with my friends."

Second: Identify your specific sin by its biblical name. Using biblical terminology lets your offender know that you realize that your offense was also a violation of God's Word and therefore a sin against Him.

Example: "Not only was I being disobedient by not obeying you, it also was selfish and inconsiderate of me."

Third: Acknowledge the harm your offense caused. Show remorse for the hurt your sin has caused.

Example: "I really am sorry that I upset you. I know that keeping my room clean is important to you. It must get old having to tell me the same thing over and over again."

Fourth: Identify an alternative biblical behavior to demonstrate repentance. One of the best ways to demonstrate to your folks that you have repented (changed your mind) is by letting them know that you have thought through a more biblical option than the one for which you are about to ask forgiveness.

Example: "I should have straightened up my room last night before I went to bed rather than playing with my Xbox."

Fifth: Ask for forgiveness. This step puts the ball in your parents' court and secures the three promises of forgiveness.

Example: "Will you forgive me?"

concerning the children, family finances, and so on). Unwillingness to discuss these things is usually a sin.

Now what about you and your folks? If they are followers of Jesus Christ, they have been given the responsibility to bring you up in the discipline and instruction of the Lord (Eph. 6:4). Since the Bible (the source of that discipline and instruction) covers every area of life, to obey this passage properly your parents must talk to you about all kinds of things—things that are easy to discuss and things that are difficult. More importantly, it's their responsibility to teach you not only how to act and speak like a Christian, but also how to think and reason like a Christian (see 1 Cor. 13:11). This means that they will have to get into your head (and your heart), and if you want to cooperate with God's program you must let them have access to it. "The purpose in a man's heart is like deep water, but a man of understanding will draw it out" (Prov. 20:5 ESV).

I would like to give two ways in which you can cooperate with this program. First, get used to the idea that your parents will sometimes have to ask you personal questions. *It's their job* to do so! Questions are the best means to get the information out of your heart. Your folks are probably not being inordinately intrusive or curious; they are just trying to do what God has told them to do. So the next time they ask you to open up, don't let pride, selfishness, fear, impatience, or laziness cause you to lock down. Avoid the shoulder shrugs and the one-word retorts. Instead, be thankful for parents who love you, and answer their questions as sincerely (and as honestly) as you know how.

My other suggestion has to do with giving your parents the information they need *without their having to ask for it*. The operative word is *initiative*. There is probably not a better way for you to earn the trust of your parents (and the freedom that comes with it) than to voluntarily give them the information they need to do their job. Don't wait for them to ask you why you are "feeling down," or "not hungry," or "not interested in going with them to wherever." Don't make them have to guess or interrogate you. Go to them. Tell them what's bugging you. Let them see what's inside. Open your heart to them. Ask for their wisdom and their prayers—maybe even for their help. Follow the instructions of the apostle Paul to the Corinthians:

We have spoken freely to you, Corinthians, and *opened wide our hearts to you*. We are not withholding our affection from you, but you are withholding yours from us. As a fair exchange—I speak as to my children—*open wide your hearts also*. (2 Cor. 6:11–13 NIV)

Disrespect

As I have already mentioned, there is probably nothing that provokes parents to anger quicker and more often than disrespect. To make matters worse, there are dozens (if not hundreds) of ways in which teens can be disrespectful to their parents. Do you remember the communication pie from the last chapter? The *words* you choose, the *tone* of your voice, and what you say with your *body*—especially your *face*—all have the potential (individually and collectively) to communicate insolence, impudence, impertinence, and contempt. I cannot possibly unpack all of these in this chapter. I will cover them more fully in chapter 11.

Lying

There is nothing you can do with your mouth that will cause you to lose more trust (and the freedom that comes with it) than lying. Two of the seven things that God says He hates in Proverbs 6:16–19 have to do with deceiving others:

> There are six things which the LORD hates,
> Yes, seven which are an abomination to Him:
> Haughty eyes, a lying tongue,
> And hands that shed innocent blood,
> A heart that devises wicked plans,
> Feet that run rapidly to evil,
> A false witness who utters lies,
> And one who spreads strife among brothers.

But what is deception?

A. Deception involves deliberately communicating to another person something that one does not believe to be true.

47

B. Deception is intentionally expressing something *outwardly* that contradicts what you believe *inwardly.*

C. Deception is deliberately misleading another person who has not been informed that he is being misled, or has not asked to be misled (as in the case of actors, illusionists, and so on, whose performances are by their very nature intentionally misleading).

There are two *basic* ways to deceive. Deception can be accomplished by falsifying or by concealing information. *Falsification* involves distorting the truth (changing the essential facts). *Concealment* involves withholding vital elements of the truth (omitting the essential facts). This is why, when American citizens are sworn in before taking the witness stand, they are told not only to tell the truth, but to tell the *whole truth* and *nothing but the truth.* These three pledges cover just about every form (and combination) of lying, except possibly for *insinuation* (which, I suppose, has been omitted from the oath for the benefit of the lawyers).

It's not enough for liars to stop lying. They must make it their goal to speak the truth in every situation.

> That, in reference to your former manner of life, you lay aside the old self, which is being corrupted in accordance with the lusts of deceit, and that you be renewed in the spirit of your mind, and put on the new self, which in the likeness of God has been created in righteousness and holiness of the truth.
>
> Therefore, *laying aside falsehood, speak truth,* each one of you, with his neighbor, for we are members of one another. (Eph. 4:22–25)

I often say to my counselees who are liars something like this: "Imagine what it will be like when some day, as you walk down the street, people will say, 'There goes John; he is the most truthful, sincere person I know.'"

"But can a person ever earn back the trust he lost as a result of lying?"

The key to earning back trust that has been lost is to habitually do the opposite of what was done to lose it. So, if you lost trust as a result of falsifying information, you must make it your goal to earn (win back) trust by accurately reporting future events. If trust was lost as a result of concealing information, you will have to earn trust by revealing things that your folks have a biblical need to know. The next time your parents ask you a question, give them more information than they can possibly want. The idea is to give them so much *relevant* and detailed information that they think to themselves (if they don't say to you), "I'm sorry I asked . . . thanks, but I really don't need that much information; I believe you already!"

If you have struggled to tell the truth, there is one more thing you will need to do: clear your conscience with (ask forgiveness of) God and with those to whom you have lied. Not only is it biblical to do so (Acts 23:1; 24:16; 1 Tim. 1:5, 19; 1 Peter 3:16), but the humility needed to correct lies that you have told in the past will be a powerful motivation not to tell any more lies in the future.

I once had to ask my little sister, who was in her early twenties at the time, to forgive me for telling her when she was a little girl that Smokey the Bear had died in a forest fire. For many years I had totally forgotten the incident, having no idea how my remarks had impacted her little life.

Remember—when you tell the truth, it may hurt someone, but the truth will not hurt him nearly as much, or as long, as telling a lie.

Grumbling and Disputing

One of the greatest indications of a person's ingratitude is the frequency with which he grumbles. God says that you shouldn't grumble at all. "Do all things without grumbling or disputing" (Phil. 2:14). The word *grumble* carries with it the idea of being dissatisfied or discontent. When you grumble to your parents, you are telling them that you are dissatisfied with them (or at least with something they have done or said). How ungrateful is that? Think of all they do for you—the sacrifices they make, the time, effort, and money that they invest in your life. Of course, since God gave you the parents He did, you are also expressing ungratefulness and discontentment to Him when you grumble about them. In what circumstances are you most likely to complain?

☐ When my parents don't buy me the things I want

☐ When my parents limit the amount of time I can spend with my friends

☑ When my parents limit my entertainment (music, movies, computer, and so on)

☐ When my parents ask me questions about my friends

☑ When my parents tell me "no" without sufficiently answering all my questions

☐ When my parents enforce my bedtime (or curfew)

☑ When my parents make decisions involving me without explaining their reasoning

Add a few of your own:

☐ When my parents _____

☐ When my parents _____

☐ When my parents _____

The word translated *disputing* in Philippians 2:14 means arguing. It suggests the idea of questionings or criticisms directed negatively toward God.[8] It includes such things as contradicting, challenging, and inappropriate questioning—bottom line: "talking back." Both of these verbal transgressions are typically rooted in the frustration (anger)[9] over not getting what one wants. Angry people are typically ungrateful, discontented individuals with a propensity to murmur and argue. In chapters 11 through 13, you will be given some biblical resources to help you express your desires to your parents without resorting to sinful forms of communication.

Entire books could be written about how to communicate biblically. The handful of insights in this little chapter are really only a start. You will probably spend much of your adult life cultivating the art and skill

8. *The MacArthur Study Bible*, New King James Version (Nashville: Word Publishing, 1997), 1824.

9. People often say they "feel frustrated." It's probably more accurate to say, "I *am* frustrated," because the emotion we *feel* when we are frustrated is anger.

of properly revealing yourself to others. If you have not already done so, now is the time to begin training yourself to be a good communicator. Remember, as a Christian, you should be a capable conversationalist. You cannot do it by yourself. But with God's Spirit teaching you from God's Word, you can learn to converse effectively not only with your parents, but with all those whom God brings across your path.

4

MAINTAINING YOUR COOL

HAVE YOU EVER wondered why you can't just turn off your feelings the way you turn off the kitchen light? Wouldn't it be nice if, after you have gotten tired of a particular feeling (such as anxiety, loneliness, depression, grief, or guilt), you could simply hit some kind of button and turn it off? Actually, it wouldn't be such a good thing if you could cut off your feelings at will. Emotions (even painful ones) play an important part in our lives. Thankfully, God didn't make our emotions so they could be easily controlled. You can't get at them or control them directly. You can only access them indirectly through your thoughts and actions.

"I'm not sure I agree with you. I'm not really comfortable with the thought that they're as difficult to get to as you seem to believe."

I understand your skepticism with this suggestion. But please allow me to persuade you by asking you a question. As you sit there reading this chapter, how frightened are you?

"Frightened?"

Yes; are you experiencing fright, panic or fear at this moment?

"What kind of question is that? I thought this was a book about anger! Why in the world would I be frightened?"

That's my point exactly. If you have no reason to *think* you are in danger, you would not *feel* frightened. Most people don't become frightened without spending a considerable amount of time *thinking* about the danger of a potentially hazardous circumstance. If you're not currently facing such a hazard, you would have to *imagine* one to become

53

frightened. Of course, if you could immediately place yourself in real danger by some *action*, you might then more easily become frightened. You see, your emotions are directly connected to your thoughts and actions. So to change your feelings you usually have to change your thoughts and your ways. (In the case of this silly example, to go from being unafraid to frightened you would have to alter your thought patterns or your physical location.) No one can instantly and permanently turn his feelings on and off at will, but you can gradually turn them around.

"All right, I guess you made your point; but what do you mean about turning feelings around?"

With the Holy Spirit's enabling power, you can develop self-control—a magnificent piece of the Spirit's fruit as identified by the apostle Paul in Galatians 5:23. By learning how to control those things that control your emotions, you can turn them around. In other words, by learning how to exercise self-control over your thoughts and actions, you can ultimately train your emotions to go in a new direction—a direction that works with you to accomplish your goals rather than against you.

WHAT IS SELF-CONTROL?

Self-control is not self-sufficiency (the ability to provide for yourself without any assistance from others; see 1 Cor. 15:10) or self-effort (see Phil. 2:12–13). It's something that the Spirit of God develops in the lives of those who are true believers in Jesus Christ. The *self* element of self-control should be viewed not as something to be held over against the Spirit's control, but as something to be held over against the necessity of being controlled (or managed) by others. The self-disciplined individual doesn't need someone else to tell him to (or make him) do what he is supposed to do (to "get up now," or "do your homework first," or "make your bed before," or "clean your room after"). From within himself (by the power of the Holy Spirit), he initiates and fulfills that which God requires of him. A person without self-control requires someone else to control (manage) his life.

In the mid-1980s, work was begun to restore and strengthen the Statue of Liberty, which for a century had withstood abuse from wind, rain, and sea. The result of the restoration was spectacular. But, if you had visited New York City during the time when the restoration was in progress, you would have been very disappointed. For several years, "Miss Liberty" was draped in hideous scaffolding that marred not only her beauty, but also the splendor of New York Harbor. During her revitalization, it was necessary to surround her with an unattractive artificial structure. For a short while, she needed help so that she could better stand on her own two feet. Sometimes, when we don't have the ability to stand on our own two feet spiritually, we may need the help of others. We may need some temporary, artificial structure in the form of additional rules, parental involvement, accountability, and even counselors (or books written by them).

Self-control is not instantly developed. As a *fruit* of the Spirit, it takes time to develop and grow to maturity. So it requires patience. Actually, both of these "fruits" must grow together. It is very difficult (if not impossible) to develop one apart from the other. You must be patient if you want to learn how to control your anger from the inside out. And, as you probably already know, lack of patience makes an angry person's short fuse even shorter.

Self-control is the ability to consistently make wise decisions and fulfill responsibilities on the basis of God's Word rather than on the basis of one's feelings. Self-control has to do with *not* giving in to your feelings. The greatest hindrance to developing self-discipline is your feelings. The greatest enemy to self-control is also your feelings. People who are self-disciplined do what the Bible says whether or not they feel like it. People without self-control do what they feel like doing (and don't do what they don't feel like doing) regardless of what the Bible says.

Self-control is largely a matter of learning how to go *against* your feelings. It is about becoming less of a feelings-oriented person and more of an obedience-oriented person.

"That is easier said than done."

It is, but you already do it to some degree.

"I do?"

Sure you do. It's Saturday morning. You went to sleep very late last night and had to get up early this morning to go with your mother on an errand with her friend. You're not particularly looking forward to this, but your mother will not let you off the hook. You're running late. You convince yourself that she hasn't been giving you enough time to hang out with *your* friends. Little by little, you begin to get on each other's nerves. You start fussing at her. She retaliates in kind. The conflict grows worse as you grow more and more impatient. The battle escalates to a full-fledged war, the likes of which neither of you have known for many years. Both of you are violating a dozen Scriptures. As the battle rages, the telephone rings. You prepare to answer it, thinking it is your mother's friend wanting to know why you're late. You pick up the receiver and sort of gruffly say, "Hello?" You then realize that it's not your mother's friend on the phone, but your friend—one with whom you have been trying to build a closer relationship for several weeks. So, in a very calm and controlled tone of voice, you pleasantly say, "Gooood Morning! . . . How are you today?" Do you see how self-controlled you can be if you really want to be?

Self-control involves not only doing but also thinking what the Bible says you should, even though you *feel* otherwise. It involves thinking about your problems in God-honoring ways even though you may feel like thinking the opposite.

That may sound like hypocrisy, but it's not hypocritical to feel one thing and do something else any more than it's hypocritical to do something loving for someone even when you don't feel like doing it. (John 3:16 doesn't say, "For God so loved the world that He felt warm and fuzzy inside.") It would be hypocrisy for you to *profess* one thing and to do (or be) another. If you say, "I'm really looking forward to going with my mother on an errand this morning" when you aren't, or "It doesn't bother me at all that I didn't get enough sleep last night" when it really does, that would be hypocrisy. But to struggle against your flesh (see Matt. 26:41; Rom. 8:5–13; Gal. 5:17) in obedience to God's Word so that your thoughts and ways may glorify Him is not hypocrisy.

Another definition of this important character quality[1] has to do with managing one's emotions. Self-control is the ability to rule one's own spirit through the power of the Holy Spirit. "He who is slow to anger is better than the mighty, and he who rules his spirit, than he who captures a city" (Prov. 16:32). Solomon says that if you can control your emotions, you are, in God's eyes, greater than a famous military leader such as General Patton or Schwarzkoph or Franks.

Solomon also warned us of the dangers associated with not being self-disciplined. "Whoever has no rule over his own spirit is like a city broken down, without walls" (Prov. 25:28 NKJV). A city without walls is vulnerable to all kinds of peril. To not control your anger is to make yourself vulnerable to such dangers as neglect of family, friends, church, school, and work activities, the development of unhealthy relationships, self-pity, guilt, and of course broken relationships with God and neighbor.

THE GUMNAZO PRINCIPLE

When I was growing up on Long Island, I was given as one of my chores the daily responsibility of sweeping the kitchen floor after supper. I was made to do this task *whether or not I felt like it*. I did it repeatedly and regularly, day in and day out, for many years. I never really enjoyed sweeping, but I went from hating it to tolerating it. As the years went by, I continued sweeping until I went to college. Finally, I was liberated from the bondage of the broom.

Many years later, I was preparing lunch in the basement kitchen of the church that had been graciously loaned to me for my first counseling office. Opening the pantry door, I discovered a pile of sugar in the middle of the closet floor. What do you suppose my next conscious thought was? If you are thinking, "Sweep it up!" you are wrong. My next conscious thought came after I had walked out the kitchen door and down a long hallway, entered a utility closet, located a broom, left the closet, and walked back down the hall again on my way to the kitchen with the broom in my hand. I thought, "Lou, what are you doing? Nobody asked you to sweep the floor.

1. For additional aspects of self-control (slices of the self-control pie), obtain a copy of the author's recording "A Biblical View of Self-Control," available at http://www.loupriolo.com.

No one is going to give you brownie points for sweeping the floor. You are sweeping the floor because it's the *right* thing to do."

The years I spent sweeping the kitchen floor as a youth as well as the subsequent discipline I had gone through since then had been used by God to develop a good habit. A habit is something practiced so frequently that it becomes "second nature." It's a routine that has become so natural that it can be performed quickly, easily, automatically, and (as in my case) unconsciously. I had, over the years, disciplined myself for the purpose of sweeping up a messy floor. Paul told Timothy, "Discipline yourself for the purpose of godliness" (1 Tim. 4:7). The word discipline (*gumnazo*—from which we get such words as *gymnastics* and *gymnasium*) means to exercise or to train.

The idea is that of a man who begins training with weights to increase his strength. The first day at the gym, he attempts to press one hundred pounds, but finds that he cannot lift the barbell above his head. Consequently, he decides to start with sixty pounds. He discovers that he can press the sixty-pound barbell 12 times over his head. He then continues to exercise with this weight for one week. The next week, he increases the barbell weight to seventy pounds. He maintains the seventy-pound weight for seven days and then graduates to eighty pounds. All the while, his muscles get stronger and larger. Week by week, he continues increasing the weight until after two years he is easily pressing over two hundred pounds. On his two-year weight-lifting anniversary, he walks over to the one-hundred-pound barbell that he could not lift above his knees on his first day of training. With one hand, he lifts that weight all the way over his head. His muscles have become so strong and so large that what was once impossible, because of training and exercise (*gumnazo*), has become easy. This is exactly what happens when we exercise ourselves for the purpose of godliness. What once seemed impossible becomes easy (second nature).

DEVELOPING HABITS

What comes to mind when you hear the word *habits*? For many, this word has negative connotations. Perhaps this is because before a person comes to Christ, the habits he develops are usually bad ones. Our sin nature and our flesh naturally predispose us to a kind of *training* that is immoral. In fact, the word *gumnazo* is used in the Bible not only for the godly kind of training but also for the ungodly. Peter, speaking of certain ungodly individuals who were somehow mingling with the true believers to whom he was writing, uses *gumnazo* to describe the development of a particular wrong habit.

> They are stains and blemishes, reveling in their deceptions, as they carouse with you, having eyes full of adultery and that never cease from sin, enticing unstable souls, having a heart *trained* [*gumnazo*] in greed, accursed children; forsaking the right way they have gone astray, having followed the way of Balaam, the son of Beor, who loved the wages of unrighteousness. (2 Peter 2:13–15)

Also, the Hebrew scholars who translated the Septuagint (the Greek version of the Old Testament from which Jesus frequently quoted) used *gumnazo* to express the same kind of habit patterns. "Can the Ethiopian change his skin or the leopard its spots? Neither can you do good who are *accustomed* to doing evil" (Jer. 13:23 NIV).

You and I have this bent toward developing sinful habits. Apart from Christ and His Word, we will develop habits to speak, act, think, and be motivated in ways that are displeasing to God. Left to our own devices, we will be filled with our own ways (see Prov. 1:30–31; 14:14). These sinful habits will also cause your parents much pain: "A child left to himself disgraces his mother" (Prov. 29:15 NIV). But with the help of the Spirit and the Scriptures, you can (and must) train yourself to think, speak, act, and be motivated biblically.

Now, if you don't already do so, I'd like to invite you to think of habits in a more positive light. The ability to form habits is truly a blessing from God for which we ought to be thankful. Habits enable us to do things comfortably, automatically, skillfully, and unconsciously.[2] Think of how complicated life would be without the ability to develop habits.

2. See Jay E. Adams, *How to Help People Change* (Grand Rapids: Zondervan, 1986), 193.

Ladies (for those of you who are old enough and whose parents allow you to wear it), imagine what it would be like if you had to put on your makeup every day without the aid of habit. Every day you would likely spend hours trying to put on your face. You'd first have to rummage through the vanity to collect just the right cosmetics from the entire collection. Next, you'd have to figure out how to open and close jars and bottles and tubes and those other unusual-shaped containers, the function of which we men can only speculate. You would have to relearn (every day) how to skillfully apply all that stuff with a dozen varieties of those funny looking applicators. Then you would have to experiment with learning to apply the exact amount, in the exact shade, in the exact places to give you the exact look you want. You would doubtless want to try at least two or three different styles (like many of you do every day with your clothing) before you were satisfied with the results. You wouldn't get to breakfast by midnight! But now, because of habit, you can perform this rather complex behavior (this creative work of art) automatically, skillfully, and unconsciously.

And you fellows, what if you couldn't remember how to operate that four-wheeler, or drive that golf ball, or cast that fly, or fire that rifle, or shoot that basketball, or worse—what if you forgot how to use the remote control? How much desire would you have to do those things if they always required the exertion of tremendous effort? Do you see how much you have been blessed because of your habits?

Thankfully, we do have the ability to develop habits. Sadly, indwelling sin makes it easy to develop bad habits. But your job as a Christian is to develop good habits.[3] Good habits are what character is all about. The more a person exercises himself for the purpose of godliness, the godlier he becomes. The godlier we become, the more we acquire the character of Christ. But this cannot be accomplished apart from the use of the Scriptures.

---

3. Let me plainly state that by using the phrase "develop good habits," I'm referring not to some sort of behavior modification technique, but rather to the process and goal of sanctification, which is produced by the Holy Spirit in conjunction with the Word of God. The change of habits I speak of are not just superficial external behaviors, such as words and actions, but they penetrate to the habits of the heart: one's thoughts and motives (see Heb. 4:12).

Now what does this have to do with anger? If you are reading this book, it's likely that for several years you have habitually responded (inwardly and outwardly) to problems with sinful anger. Now you are learning to change. What you want to change, however, is a habit. So you will have to rehabituate yourself to do things differently. Moreover, unlike your unbelieving friends who simply try to break their habits, as a Christian you must exchange a bad habit for a good one. That's the way the Bible says Christians are to change.

In Proverbs 28:13 we find an interesting word: "He who conceals his transgressions will not prosper, but he who confesses and *forsakes* them will find compassion." The Hebrew word for "forsake" (*azab*) is quite strong. It means to let go of, leave, forsake, or abandon. Sin must be left behind, abandoned, and forsaken.

The concept of forsaking or letting go of sin corresponds to the New Testament idea of "putting off" sin. This is the first half of a twofold process essential for change. The second part of the process is "putting on" the biblical alternative to the sin habit we are trying to remove from our lives. I have previously outlined the put off / put on dynamic in another book.[4]

ZAP THEOLOGY: THE KISS AND MAKE UP WITH GOD SYNDROME

Have you ever struggled to overcome a bad habit in your life? Sure you have! We all have. When many Christians "struggle" with sin, however, they don't really struggle at all. Rather, they simply confess their sin to God, pray that He will help them change, and promptly get off their knees, expecting that God has somehow infused ("zapped") them with a special measure of grace that will enable them to never commit the same sin again, without any (or with very little) further effort on their part. This is what is sometimes referred to as "the kiss and make up with God syndrome."[5]

4. Lou Priolo, The *Complete Husband* (Amityville, NY: Calvary Press, 1999), 160–61.
5. This term was used by Jay Adams in various lectures and personal conversations I've had the pleasure of having with him.

Progressive sanctification (how a Christian over time becomes transformed into the image of Christ) is, of course, an act of God, but it's also a process that requires our cooperation. It's not enough merely to pray that God will change us. We must also *do* what the Bible says is necessary to "put off" the sin and to "put on" Christ. Change is a twofold process for the Christian. We actually put off our sin by putting on its biblical alternative. To put it another way, Christians don't "break" habits—pagans do. Christians replace bad habits with good ones.

It's not enough for the Christian who habitually lies to simply stop lying. He must make it his goal to become truthful. "Therefore, laying aside falsehood, speak truth, each one of you, with his neighbor, for we are members of one another" (Eph. 4:25). It's not enough for a thief to simply stop stealing. He must not only put off *stealing*, but he must also put on *diligence* and *generosity*. "Let him who steals steal no longer; but rather let him labor, performing with his own hands what is good, in order that he may have something to share with him who has need" (Eph. 4:28).

This put off / put on dynamic can happen only as the mind is renewed through Scripture.

> That, in reference to your former manner of life, you lay aside the old self, which is being corrupted in accordance with the lusts of deceit, *and that you be renewed in the spirit of your mind*, and put on the new self, which in the likeness of God has been created in righteousness and holiness of the truth. (Eph. 4:22–24)

The Word of God is necessary to produce lasting change in your life. The Holy Spirit takes the Scriptures you have internalized (through Bible reading, study, memorization, meditation, and so on) and changes (transforms) you from the inside. "And do not be conformed to this world, but be transformed by the renewing of your mind, that you may prove what the will of God is, that which is good and acceptable and perfect" (Rom. 12:2). You cannot properly be sanctified apart from God's Word.

So it will not be enough for you to simply learn how to stop getting angry—to control your temper. You must also learn how to be gentle and kind and forgiving.

> Let all bitterness and wrath and anger and clamor and slander be put away from you, along with all malice. And be kind to one another, tender-hearted, forgiving each other, just as God in Christ also has forgiven you. (Eph. 4:31–32)

In the next chapter, we will unpack these two verses as we examine how to handle rejection and hurt.

5

HOW TO HANDLE REJECTION AND HURT[1]

Let all bitterness, wrath, anger, clamor, and evil speaking
be put away from you, with all malice. (Eph. 4:31 NKJV)

LET'S "ZOOM OUT" for a moment and look at your responses to rejection with a wide-angle lens. How do you usually respond when you are rejected or hurt by others besides your parents?

Each of us desires certain expressions of love, such as respect, appreciation, approval, praise, and commendation. The Bible assumes that each of us naturally finds a certain measure of delight in these things. The problem occurs, however, when we delight in them too much.

When you are rejected or hurt, ask yourself, "Did this person really sin against me? Is what he did to me really a sin in God's eyes?" If someone has sinned against you, there are two options available to you. You may choose to overlook it or to cover it in love (see Prov. 17:9; 1 Peter 4:8). If you are unable to overlook it, the other option is to follow Luke 17:3: "If your brother sins against you, rebuke him; and if he repents, forgive him" (NKJV). That is, pursue your offender with the intent of

1. The material in this chapter has been adapted from my book *Picking Up the Pieces* (Phillipsburg, NJ: P&R Publishing, 2012), 87–104.

65

granting him forgiveness when he acknowledges his sin. But if you were hurt as a result of that which was not a sin, you must repent of your unbiblical (proud) thinking that caused you to be too easily offended (over something that didn't offend the Lord).

In Ephesians 4:31, the apostle Paul identified six sinful ways in which people tend to respond in the midst of relationship difficulties.

SINFUL RESPONSES TO REJECTION

The first response is *bitterness*. This word literally describes the bitter taste of certain food and drink. The verb translated "to be bitter" means "to cut" or "to prick." You may think of the word *bitterness* as an inward resentment or an unforgiving spirit, and so it is. But this inward attitude will cut and prick others as well. "See to it that no one comes short of the grace of God; that no root of bitterness springing up causes trouble, and by it *many* be defiled" (Heb. 12:15).

Bitterness is the result of not forgiving others. If you are bitter toward someone, it's an indication that you haven't truly forgiven that person.

The second response is *wrath*. This word has a broad range of meaning. Its most basic meaning has to do with "a vital force." It is heated, passionate, furious anger that quickly boils up and almost as quickly subsides. This is a sudden outburst of anger—like a firecracker that explodes once and then is spent. When a person responds with this kind of anger, doors may be slammed, feet may stomp, people may be punched or kicked, items may be thrown and broken, voices may be raised, names may be hurled, unrighteous expletives may be used, and false accusations may abound.

A good example of this overactive and volatile anger is found in the second chapter of Matthew. The following Scripture passage is the account of the magi who were following a special star that was to lead them to baby Jesus.

> Then Herod secretly called the magi, and ascertained from them the time the star appeared. And he sent them to Bethlehem, and said,

"Go and make careful search for the Child; and when you have found Him, report to me, that I too may come and worship Him." And having heard the king, they went their way. . . . And having been warned by God in a dream not to return to Herod, they departed for their own country by another way. . . .

Then when Herod saw that he had been *tricked* by the magi, he became *very enraged*, and sent and *slew all the male children* who were in Bethlehem and in all its environs, from two years old and under, according to the time which he had ascertained from the magi. (Matt. 2:7–9, 12, 16)

Anger is the third descriptive word used in Ephesians 4:31. It has two basic meanings.

The more general and broad meaning is a burst of emotion that sometimes manifests itself in impulsive actions—especially vindictive ones. It's a strong feeling that produces not only impulsivity, but also intense passion—outward expressions of displeasure and anger. This intense passion can be quite powerful and destructive. It's much easier to act impulsively right after being hurt or rejected than it is in more pleasant circumstances.

The more specific meaning of this word is a less explosive but more enduring kind of anger. This is a state of mind or a condition of the soul. It's the kind of anger that, if left unchecked, produces the characterological anger that we looked at earlier and turns its possessor into an angry man. This kind of anger is the slow boil variety.

When a person with this kind of anger is hurt or rejected, he doesn't usually react violently. In fact, he may even withdraw. When you ask him if he is angry, he may well respond with, "No, I'm just a little *hurt*." This kind of internalized anger can be so subtle that you may have a difficult time detecting it in your own heart.

The fourth common response to being rejected is *clamor*. This is a public outcry, a tumult. (The verb means "to croak.") The person who is clamoring is griping, complaining, and bellyaching in a rabble-rousing, agitating sort of way. There is a vivid illustration of the effects of this kind of public instigation in the book of Acts.

And about that time there arose *no small disturbance*[2] concerning the Way. For a certain man named Demetrius, a silversmith, who made silver shrines of Artemis, was bringing no little business to the craftsmen; these he *gathered together*[3] with the workmen of similar trades, and said, "Men, you know that our prosperity depends upon this business. And you see and hear that not only in Ephesus, but in almost all of Asia, this Paul has persuaded and turned away a considerable number of people, saying that gods made with hands are no gods at all. And not only is there danger that this trade of ours fall into disrepute, but also that the temple of the great goddess Artemis be regarded as worthless and that she whom all of Asia and the world worship should even be dethroned from her magnificence." And when they heard this and were *filled with rage*, they began crying out, saying, "Great is Artemis of the Ephesians!" And the city was *filled with the confusion.* (Acts 19:23–29)

The fifth item in our text is *slander* or *evil speaking*. The Greek word (*blasphemia*) carries the concept of hurt, injury, or harm with speech. This term involves speech that is abusive, defaming, or harmful to another's good name. It is used to describe the strongest form of mockery or slander. Whereas clamor speaks of a more public form of criticism, slander or evil speaking may occur between as few as two people.

What have you told others about those who hurt you? Have you been guilty of clamor or gossip? I realize that those persons may have done you much wrong, but you should not respond in kind. The apostle Peter said,

> To sum up, all of you be harmonious, sympathetic, brotherly, kind-hearted, and humble in spirit; not returning evil for evil or insult for insult, but giving a blessing instead; for you were called for the very purpose that you might inherit a blessing.
>
> For,

"THE ONE WHO DESIRES LIFE, TO LOVE AND SEE GOOD DAYS,
MUST KEEP HIS TONGUE FROM EVIL AND HIS LIPS FROM SPEAKING DECEIT.

2. This is an introductory summary statement that identifies the result of the clamor before explaining its exact nature.

3. Note the public gathering of those whom Demetrius intended to infect with his bitterness.

He must turn away from evil and do good;
He must seek peace and pursue it." (1 Peter 3:8–11)

The last item on our list is *malice*. The word has a variety of meanings, including maliciousness, hatred, resentment, ill feeling, ill will, and the desire to injure. Malice holds grudges. Herodias had this kind of malice for John the Baptist. The hatred she held against him for condemning her unbiblical marriage to Herod ultimately manifested itself in murder. "And Herodias had a grudge against him and wanted to put him to death and could not do so" (Mark 6:19).

The Greek word for "had a grudge against" can also be translated "held it against" or "had it in for." If you're holding something against someone or somehow "have it in for" him, you may be flirting with malice.

So which kind of anger best describes your response to being hurt or rejected? Do you resemble a bitter root, a firecracker, a pot of boiling water, a public croaker, or a grudge holder?

"OK, I confess; I'm guilty of at least one or two of these. So what do I do now?"

Keep reading! The biblical solution to these problems is found in the next verse, Ephesians 4:32: "And be kind to one another, tenderhearted, forgiving one another, just as God in Christ also forgave you" (NKJV). This verse prescribes three antidotes to venomous anger. It provides three biblical imperatives for us to follow when we've been hurt or rejected by others.

The first response is to be *kind*. The word means to be good, pleasant, merciful, and generous. Kindness encompasses the idea of loving one's enemies, doing good, and lending without expecting repayment. It's being merciful even to those who have hurt us.

> But I say to you who hear: *Love* your enemies, *do good* to those who hate you, *bless* those who curse you, and *pray* for those who spitefully use you. To him who strikes you on the one cheek, *offer* the other also. And from him who takes away your cloak, *do not withhold* your tunic either. *Give* to everyone who asks of you. And

from him who takes away your goods *do not ask them back*. And just as you want men to do to you, you also *do to them likewise*. But if you love those who love you, what credit is that to you? For even sinners love those who love them. And if you do good to those who do good to you, what credit is that to you? For even sinners do the same. And if you lend to those from whom you hope to receive back, what credit is that to you? For even sinners lend to sinners to receive as much back. But *love* your enemies, *do good*, and *lend*, hoping for nothing in return; and your reward will be great, and you will be sons of the Highest. For He is *kind* to the unthankful and evil. Therefore be *merciful*, just as your Father also is merciful. (Luke 6:27–36 NKJV)

In this passage, Christ gives a general order: "Love your enemies." In verses 27 and 28, He gives specific applications of that general order.

Application #1: "Do good to those who hate you."
Application #2: "Bless those who curse you."
Application #3: "Pray for those who mistreat you."

He continues giving specific applications of this general command in verses 29 through 31:

Application #4: "Whoever hits you on the cheek, offer him the other also."
Application #5: "Whoever takes away your coat, do not withhold your shirt from him either."
Application #6: "Give to everyone who asks of you, and whoever takes away what is yours, do not demand it back."
Application #7: "Just as you want people to treat you, treat them in the same way." (This is a rule of thumb for loving your enemies.)

So, in order to show kindness to the one who has hurt you, you must love him, do good to him, pray for him, praise him (when you can), turn the other cheek to him, go the second mile with him, and give him what he needs. In other words, treat him exactly the way that you would want him to treat you. And if you do, no matter what happens here on earth, your reward will be great in heaven.

TRY A LITTLE TENDERHEARTEDNESS

The next word in our text is *tenderhearted*. A compound term that combines the word for "good" with the word for "guts" or "inward parts," it means "full of compassion" or "having pity." It suggests a warm, tender feeling toward others:

> Finally, all of you be of one mind, having compassion for one another; love as brothers, *be tenderhearted*, be courteous; *not returning evil for evil or reviling for reviling, but on the contrary blessing,* knowing that you were called to this, that you may inherit a blessing. (1 Peter 3:8–9 NKJV)

The context in which Peter uses the word *tenderhearted* is one of being offended. The person who is tenderhearted can look at his offenders much like Christ looked at His, focusing more on their needs than on His own. The tenderhearted person has compassion for the one who offended him because he realizes that the very sin that hurt him is probably hurting his offender even more.[4] Have you ever thought about your offenders with such compassion? A tenderhearted person is able to focus his thoughts and energy on ministering to his offender rather than on getting even with him.

We now come to what may be for you the most important part in this book: Bible basics about forgiveness. The opposite of forgiveness is not anger; it's bitterness. The more you hate those who offend you, the more bitter and resentful you will become. And then you'll find yourself getting angrier more often than if you'd forgiven.

---

4. "Do not be deceived, God is not mocked; for whatever a man sows, this he will also reap" (Gal. 6:7). We cannot continuously sin without experiencing consequences. Those who regularly offend us are in all likelihood experiencing the consequences of their sinful actions even though they might not yet recognize them.

Bitterness is the result of responding improperly to a hurt: "See to it that no one comes short of the grace of God; that no root of bitterness springing up causes trouble, and by it many be defiled" (Heb. 12:15).

The Scripture says that bitterness is like a root. Roots have to be planted. When someone hurts you,[5] it's as if a seed has been dropped onto the soil of your heart. You can choose to respond in two ways. You can either pluck out the seed by forgiving your offender, or you can begin to cultivate the seed by reviewing the hurt over and over in your mind. Bitterness is the result of dwelling too long on a hurt. It's the result of not truly forgiving an offender (see Matt. 18:34–35).

Janie's best friend, Abby, had been planning a sleepover for all the girls in the youth group. All summer long, the party was the topic of discussion. Everyone was going to be there. Three days before the sleepover, Janie found out that some old family friends were coming over the weekend of the party. Although Abby's party had been scheduled months before, Janie's dad wanted her to drop her "silly little party plans" and stay at home with the family friends. Janie knew that all the popular people would be at the sleepover, in addition to all her friends. Plus, Janie made a commitment to the party long before she even knew about her father's plans. Janie's father insisted that she stay home. He has just dropped the seed of hurt onto the soil of her heart.

Janie's seed of hurt could be easily transformed into a root of bitterness.

Regardless of what your offenders have done to hurt you, as a Christian who is committed to pleasing God, you really have no choice but to forgive them of any sins they have committed against you.

---

5. The hurt can be real or imagined; it makes no difference. The result is the same. If you do not deal with it biblically, you will become bitter. If I hurt you as a result of my sin and you choose not to overlook it or cover it in love (Prov. 17:9; 1 Peter 4:8), you must follow Luke 17:3 and pursue me with the intent of granting me forgiveness, and I must repent. If you get your feelings hurt as a result of something I did that was not a sin, you must repent of your unbiblical thinking that caused you to be offended at something that was not a sin.

Janie's Internal Thoughts	Cultivation of Janie's Bitterness
"I can't believe he's doing this to me! I've been planning to go to this sleepover all summer long."	Janie presses the seed an inch or two into the soil of her heart.
"He's so selfish. All he thinks about is what he wants."	Janie covers the seed with more soil.
"He is never willing to let me have fun when his plans might be upset."	Janie aerates the soil.
"Why did I get stuck with a father like him?"	Janie waters the seed.
"He's such a jerk!"	Janie fertilizes her hurt and it starts to sprout.
"I can't wait until I can get out of here. Then nobody will be able to spoil my fun."	Janie weeds her little sprout, and its roots grow deeper.
"He can't do this to me. I'm going to give him a taste of his own medicine. I'm going to embarrass him so badly, he'll wish that he had sent me to the sleepover in a limousine."	Janie builds a greenhouse around her stinkweed and starts charging people admission to see it.

BIBLE BASICS ABOUT FORGIVENESS

The principles that follow are based on Luke 17:3–10. Other passages have been cited where applicable.

"Take heed to yourselves. If your brother sins against you, rebuke him; and if he repents, forgive him. And if he sins against you seven times in a day, and seven times in a day returns to you, saying, 'I repent,' you shall forgive him."

And the apostles said to the Lord, "Increase our faith."

So the Lord said, "If you have faith as a mustard seed, you can say to this mulberry tree, 'Be pulled up by the roots and be planted in the sea,' and it would obey you. And which of you, having a servant plowing or tending sheep, will say to him when he has come in from the field, 'Come at once and sit down to eat'? But will he not rather say to him, 'Prepare something for my supper, and gird yourself and serve me till I have eaten and drunk, and afterward you will eat and drink'? Does he thank that servant because he did the things that were commanded him? I think not. So likewise you, when you have done all those things which you are commanded, say, 'We are unprofitable servants. We have done what was our duty to do.' " (NKJV)

1. Forgiveness is to be granted only if a sin has been committed against you.

Jesus said, "If your brother sins . . ." He didn't say, "If he doesn't give you what you want," "If he lets you down," "If he hurts your feelings," or "If he profoundly disappoints you." Your brother (who may also be one of your parents) may do any and all of these things in the process of sinning, but he is not in need of your forgiveness unless he sins against you.[6]

2. Sometimes the offended party must initiate forgiveness.

If you cannot overlook the transgression (Prov. 19:11) or cover it in love (1 Peter 4:8), you are obligated as a Christian to go to a brother who has sinned against you and to "rebuke him." Sometimes we must go to our sinning brother and tell him about his sin with the intention of being able to grant him forgiveness. I realize that this may present a particular problem for a teenager who must approach his believing parent who has sinned. In chapter 13, "How to Talk to Your Parents about Their Sin," we will unpack Luke 17:3 a bit more.

"But he sinned against me! Why does his sin obligate me to go to him? Didn't Jesus say somewhere that he is supposed to come to me before he brings his gift to the altar?"

He did. In Matthew 5:23, Jesus tells us to seek forgiveness from those we have offended. In that passage the *offending* party is told to go.

---

6. Proud ("oversensitive") people are especially prone to perceiving nonsinful pinpricks as though they were being stabbed through the heart.

But we are looking at Luke 17, which says the *offended* party should go. Since you, as the offended party, are the one who has knowledge of the wrong, you are to go. The one who knows about the offense is the one who goes. Perhaps your offender doesn't know about his sin, or maybe he doesn't want to seek reconciliation. Or, as happens rather frequently, it could be that there is a misperception on someone's part that requires a discussion to clear up the issue. It might even be discovered that no real sin was actually committed.

3. Forgiveness is fundamentally a promise.

In his insightful book *From Forgiven to Forgiving*, Dr. Jay Adams explains,

> When God forgives, He goes on record. He says so. He declares, "I will not remember your sins" (Isa. 43:25; see also Jer. 31:34). Isn't that wonderful? When He forgives, God lets us know that He will no longer hold our sins against us. If forgiveness were merely an emotional experience, we would not know that we were forgiven. But praise God, we do, because forgiveness is a process at the end of which God declares that the matter of sin has been dealt with once for all. [7]

Now what is that declaration? What does God do when He goes on record saying that our sins are forgiven? He makes a promise. Forgiveness is not a feeling; forgiveness is a *promise!*

When you forgive, you are promising to no longer hold your offender's trespasses against him. You are also promising to impute your forgiveness to him (much like Christ imputed His righteousness to you when you became a Christian). The dictionary defines *impute* as follows: (1) "to charge with the fault or responsibility for"; (2) "to attribute or credit."[8] When you promise not to impute your offender's trespasses against him, you are promising to no longer charge him for what he has done. This means you are not going to allow yourself to

7. Jay E. Adams, *From Forgiven to Forgiving: Learning to Forgive One Another God's Way* (Amityville, NY: Calvary Press, 1994), 11-12.
8. *American Heritage Dictionary of the English Language*, 3rd ed., s.v. "impute."

dwell on the offense. You will refuse to cultivate those seeds of hurt, but rather will immediately pluck them out of the soil of your heart.

When you promise to impute your forgiveness, you commit to make every effort to think well of him, to pray for him, and to speak well of him, if possible. These two promises can be made in the form of a personal commitment in your heart even if your offender does not acknowledge his sins to you. This is what is sometimes referred to as "forgiving someone in your heart" (see Mark 11:25).

If he does acknowledge his sins and asks for your forgiveness, you will make those promises to him as you verbally grant him forgiveness. In such cases, you will be making him two additional promises. The "not remembering his sins" concept is an implicit promise never to bring up the offense to him again. If you have forgiven him, there is no need to discuss it again. Similar sins that he may commit in the future may require new confrontations. In addition, when you verbally grant someone forgiveness, you are promising not to tell anyone else about the offense.[9]

4. Forgiveness is not the same as trust.

If someone sins against you, it's incumbent upon you as a Christian to forgive that person as you have been forgiven by God in Christ (see Matt. 18:21–35). However, it's incumbent upon that person to earn back the trust he lost as a result of his sin. Forgiveness should be immediate. Trust may take time. To withhold trust after it has been earned is unloving since "love believes all things" (1 Cor. 13:7; see also Prov. 27:22; Jer. 13:23; Matt. 25:14–31; Luke 16:10–12). But whether or not you are able to trust your offender quickly, you must trust God to work through him (especially if he is a parent) and to protect you from danger.

5. Forgiveness involves an act of the will—not the emotions.

If your offender repents, you must forgive him—on the spot. Jesus phrased this in such a way as to make it clear that, in the absence of

---

9. If other individuals have a biblical need to know about the offense, you can lovingly urge the offender to confess to all necessary parties so that you will not be obligated to disclose anything to anyone.

evidence to the contrary, you have to take your offender at his word and grant him forgiveness. Even if it's the seventh time in one day he has asked you to do so, you are to forgive him (Luke 17:4).[10] Jesus does not give you very much time to get your feelings in line *before* you forgive. You are to do it as an act of your will in obedience to God. Your feelings will follow. If you wait until your feelings change before you forgive, you may never obey the Lord's command.

In Luke 17:5–10, the disciples had a hard time with Christ's teaching on this subject. Their response to Him was an incredulous, "Increase our faith" (v. 5). They thought they needed more faith in order to obey this teaching. Through a parable, Christ instructed them that it was not more faith they needed, but rather more faithfulness. The slave in the story was not being asked to do something he was incapable of doing, despite how exhausted he might have *felt* after returning to his master's house from a long day's work. Preparing the evening meal was something he was expected to do. It was not optional. Neither was it something for which he would be receiving time-and-a-half pay for working overtime. He couldn't even expect to receive special commendation. It was his job! Forgiveness is a part of your job description too. Like any job, some responsibilities are easier and more enjoyable than others. Some you feel like doing; others you do whether or not you feel like doing them.

"But what if *after* I forgive them, I begin to have feelings of resentment toward them? I'll feel like such a hypocrite!"

You will not feel that way if you think biblically about the matter. After granting forgiveness, remind yourself that you made a promise to your offender. Don't let that seed of hurt develop into a root of bitterness by dwelling on it. Pray for him and put your mind into a Philippians 4:8 thought pattern: "Whatever things are true, whatever things are noble, whatever things are just, whatever things are pure, whatever things are lovely, whatever things are of good report, if there is any virtue and if there is anything praiseworthy—meditate on these things" (NKJV).

---

10. This is not to say that *for his sake* you cannot call into question (urge him to examine) the sincerity of his repentance before you grant him forgiveness.

Rather than reviewing hurtful mental images from the past, or laying vindictive plans for the future (seeing the face of your offender on a dartboard, or on a baseball you are about to pulverize with your "Louisville Slugger"), picture his face with the words "I've forgiven you" boldly imprinted across the image. Put your imagination to work on Philippians 4:8 (or on other relevant passages of Scripture). You may be surprised at how much better you will feel, as well as how quickly you will forget, once you truly forgive. Forgetting is the result of forgiving, not the means of it. It's the final step of the process, not the first one.

PROVOCATIVE PARENTS

LET ME TAKE YOU back into my counseling office for a moment to continue the conversation I was having with Jim and Linda (Joshua's parents). To remind you where we left off, having tentatively diagnosed Joshua as possessing characterological anger (of qualifying, in other words, for the dubious distinction of being an *angry man*), I asked Jim and Linda another question. "Can you think of a verse in the Bible that addresses angry children?"

"Yes: 'Fathers, do not provoke your children to anger,' " Jim said, as the expression on his face changed from confidence that he knew the right answer to dismay that he and Linda might somehow be guilty of provoking Joshua.

"That's right," I explained. "Ephesians 6:4 says that rather than provoking your children, you should 'bring them up in the discipline and instruction of the Lord.' Also in a parallel passage, Colossians 3:21, Paul uses a different word to express the same idea: 'Fathers, do not exasperate your children, that they may not lose heart [or be discouraged].' "

WHO'S TO BLAME?

At this point, I had to remind Jim and Linda that I was not a Freudian psychologist who was going to blame them for their child's problems.

"You two are big sinners. Joshua is a little sinner. As a sinner, he must assume one hundred percent responsibility for his anger problem.

God expects him not to be sinfully angry, regardless of how his parents provoke him. God expects him to change whether or not you choose to change. But the two of you are responsible before God not to contribute to Joshua's anger problem. To the degree that you are provoking him to anger, you must stop. To that same degree you can make it easier for Joshua to correct his anger problem."

The rest of the first counseling session (with corresponding homework assignments), as well as the next two sessions, were devoted to identifying and removing those parental provocations that were probably affecting Joshua's behavior. Parents do lots of things to push the buttons of their children. The original book that I wrote for parents contains twenty-five common ways that parents tend to provoke their children to anger. In this book, I will cover only seventeen of them—the ones that relate most to teens.

Before you continue, I want to emphasize again that if you are a Christian, you can learn to change your behavior (i.e., control your anger) regardless of what your parents do to push your buttons. Would it be easier for you to change if they learned how to obey the Bible better by not provoking you? Almost certainly it would. But you may or may not be able to successfully motivate them to change. So I provide you with this list in the hope that you can encourage your parents to read this chapter and to discuss these potential provocations with you. (If they have read my original book, they should already be acquainted with them.) I have removed *some* of the parental instructions that appear in that version. Where I have left them in, it's either because I believe them to be applicable to you or so that you may have a basis for discussing these with your parents. In some cases, I will provide instructions (and/or biblical alternatives) for you to follow when you've been provoked.

COMMON WAYS PARENTS CAN PROVOKE THEIR CHILDREN TO ANGER

1. By Lacking Marital Harmony

In my opinion, parents who do not live with each other in harmony are at the greatest risk for provoking anger in their children. "For this cause a man shall leave his father and his mother, and shall cleave to his wife; and they shall become one flesh" (Gen. 2:24).

The verse above appears four and a half times in the Bible. If a husband and wife do not develop the "one flesh" intimacy intended by God, other problems develop over time. Of these, one of the most common is that each spouse is tempted to develop a deeper level of intimacy with something or someone else other than his or her spouse. Typically, the husband develops closer ties with people at work or play (or with his work or hobby itself). The wife, characteristically, develops an unhealthy relationship with the children. Once this occurs, it's usually just a matter of time before the home becomes "child-centered."

Another correlation between lack of marital harmony and children who struggle with anger is the defiling effect that bitterness has on them. As you observe any resentment that may exist due to your parents' lack of harmony, you become more susceptible to acquiring those bitter thoughts, motives, attitudes, and actions that you have seen and heard modeled by them. Look again at Hebrews 12:15: "See to it that no one comes short of the grace of God; that no root of bitterness springing up causes trouble, and by it many be defiled." The "many" most likely to be defiled when your folks are bitter at each other are you and your siblings. Remember also that bitterness is one of the links in the developmental chain from anger to rebellion. If you, by God's grace, can keep yourself from developing bitterness (and, as we learned in the last chapter, learn to forgive), you will have gone a long way toward preventing the characterological anger and rebellion that this book was written to correct.

2. By Establishing and Maintaining a Child-centered Home

Another illustration that I used with Jim and Linda pinpointed what was at the heart of Joshua's anger.

"I'm going to draw a model of two drastically different families. When I'm through, I would like for you to tell me which of the two models best represents your family. The first family revolves around the children. It's a child-centered home. A child-centered home is one in which a child believes, and is allowed to behave as though, the entire household—parents and siblings (and pets)—exist for one purpose: *to please him.*"

A child-centered home is one in which the children are allowed to commit the following indiscretions:

- To interrupt adults when they are talking
- To use manipulation and rebellion to get their way
- To dictate family schedule (including mealtimes, bedtimes, and so on)
- To take precedence over the needs of the spouse
- To have an equal or overriding vote in all decision-making matters
- To demand excessive time and attention from parents to the exclusion of the parents' other biblical responsibilities
- To escape the consequences of their sinful and irresponsible behavior
- To speak to parents as though they were peers
- To be the dominant influence in the home
- To be entertained and coddled (rather than disciplined) out of a bad mood

A child (or teenager) who is at the center of a child-centered home believes that he and his desires should be the focal point of the entire household. Is this how you picture your place in your home?

A God-Centered Home. "On the other hand," I told Jim and Linda, "a God-centered home is a home that is patterned after Genesis 2:24. Virtually all marriage and family problems can be traced back to a failure to leave one's parents, cleave to one's spouse, or become one flesh with one's spouse."

When two people leave their respective homes to establish a new home for Christ, they become a family *before any children arrive.* When children are added, mother and father function as the decision-making heads of the expanding family unit. This unit is not a democracy. Your father is the head of this unit, and your mother is his helper. The two are one flesh.

As you and your siblings were born, you were welcomed into the family, but not as a part of the decision-making corps of that unit. In other words, you certainly are part of your family, a very important part, but you are *not one flesh* with your parents. You never were. You never will be.

When parents do not establish a home that is clearly Christ-centered (one in which each member understands his biblical role in the family and is committed to please Christ more than self), it's likely that the home will become child-centered. If a husband and wife do not work at being closer to each other than to any and all of their children, the children may view themselves as equal in authority to, rather than as subordinate to, them. In such "democratic" households, children tend to become angry when their desires do not get placed on "equal status" with the desires of their parents. Can you relate? If so, you may have to change the way you view your position as a member of the family into which God has placed you. (And you may have to do so whether or not your folks change their perspective.)

According to Scripture, the relationship between husband and wife is a permanent relationship that is not to be broken (Matt. 19:3–6). The authority/submission relationship between parents and their children is a temporary one, which eventually *is* to be broken according to Genesis 2:24. Therefore, the relationship between a husband and wife is the *priority* relationship. The relationships between parents and children and between siblings are important, but *secondary*.

The concept of a God-centered home is derived from the biblical principle that the purpose of every Christian is to glorify God (1 Cor. 6:20; 10:31). In contrast to a child-centered home, where pleasing and serving the child is the dominant theme, the God-centered home is one in which everyone is committed to pleasing and serving God. God's desires are exalted over those of everyone else.

After these two models were explained to Jim and Linda, I asked them to identify the pattern that best described their home most often. They chose the child-centered home, as have the overwhelming majority of parents of angry children I've asked over the years.

Which model best describes your household: the child-centered or the God-centered home?

Child-Centered	God-Centered
I believe that my entire family exists to please me and make me happy.	I believe that the husband is the head of the family, and the wife is to be submissive to him. Theirs is the primary relationship. It's intended to be permanent and exists to glorify God. My relationship with my parents is subsequent to their relationship with each other.

You may or may not be able to (or need to) change your parents' mind about this matter, but, as I have said, you can change your own.

3. By Modeling Sinful Anger

You have already learned about the volcano and the clam. And you probably remember this passage:

> Do not associate with a man given to anger;
> Or go with a hot-tempered man,
> Lest you learn his ways,
> And find a snare for yourself. (Prov. 22:24–25)

When you are constantly bombarded by expressions of sinful anger, you may soon come to the conclusion that the only way to solve problems is to *win*. This, of course, is not biblical. If you are a Christian, you don't have to let the anger of others rub off on you. Put yourself in your parents' place. Try to determine a more biblical way to handle the problem (if you know what it is) than by getting angry. Pray for an opportunity to share that alternative respectfully with them. (You will gain some insight on how to do this effectively in chapter 13.)

4. By Consistently Disciplining in Anger

> O LORD, rebuke me not in Thy wrath;
> And chasten me not in Thy burning anger. (Ps. 38:1)

84

When your parents are angry, it's easier for them to overdiscipline you. You may be tempted to interpret such anger as a personal attack. If you do view their discipline as such an attack, you will likely have done so only after concluding that your parents' motive for the discipline is *vindictive* (they wanted to pay you back for the misery your offense caused them personally) rather than *corrective* (they wanted to help you to make the changes in your life that would be pleasing to God). The thing is, you don't have the ability to read your parents' thoughts and motives, so you don't really know for sure what they are thinking. If you prematurely (without asking them) conclude that their discipline is punitive rather than redemptive, you violate 1 Corinthians 4:5 (which forbids you to judge their motives) and will find it difficult not to get angry. You would do better to set your mind on evaluating whether you are somehow responsible for provoking your parents to the anger you are experiencing.

5. By Scolding

> And while [Jesus] was in Bethany at the home of Simon the leper, and reclining at the table, there came a woman with an alabaster vial of very costly perfume of pure nard; and she broke the vial and poured it over His head. But some were indignantly remarking to one another, "Why has this perfume been wasted? For this perfume might have been sold for over three hundred denarii, and the money given to the poor." And they were *scolding* her. (Mark 14:3–5)

One of the Greek words from which the term *scolding* was derived means "to snort with anger." It was used to describe the snorting of horses. In his book *Hints on Child Training*, first published in 1891, H. Clay Trumbull (who, by the way, is considered by many to be the founder of Sunday school), explains,

> To "scold" is to assail or revile with boisterous speech. The word itself seems to have a primary meaning akin to that of barking or howling. . . .
> Scolding is always an expression of a bad spirit and of a loss of temper. . . . The essence of the scolding is in the multiplication of hot words in expression of strong feelings that, while eminently natural,

ought to be held in better control. . . . It is scolding in the one case as in the other; and scolding is never in order. . . .

No parent ought to talk to a child while that parent is unable to talk in a natural tone of voice, and with carefully measured words. If the parent is tempted to speak rapidly, or to multiply words without stopping to weigh them, or to show an excited state of feeling, the parent's first duty is to gain entire self-control. Until that control is secured, there is no use of the parent's trying to attempt any measure of child training. The loss of self-control is for the time being an utter loss of power for the control of others.[1]

If your parents scold you, bear patiently with them. Don't roll your eyes (or visibly respond with other manifestations of disdain). Listen to what they are saying. They are probably saying the right thing in the wrong way. Ask the Lord to show you any truth that you need to apply to your life. Agree with your parents where you can. Then afterwards, probably in an entirely different conversation, the Lord may give you an opportunity to respectfully talk to them about the scolding. Appendix B, "How to Respond to Reproof," is included to help you better respond when others (properly or improperly) reprimand you.

6. By Being Inconsistent with Discipline

Therefore, I was not vacillating when I intended to do this, was I? Or that which I purpose, do I purpose according to the flesh, that with me there should be yes, yes and no, no at the same time? But as God is faithful, our word to you is not yes and no. (2 Cor. 1:17–18)

Because the sentence against an evil deed is not executed quickly, therefore the hearts of the sons of men among them are given fully to do evil. (Eccl. 8:11)

Parents discipline inconsistently in two common ways. The first is by having different parental standards of discipline. For example, father spanks and mother talks. Father believes that a certain behavior is wrong.

---

1. H. Clay Trumbull, *Hints on Child-Training* (Philadelphia: John D. Wattles & Co., 1893), 217–19.

Mother sees nothing wrong with that same behavior. As a rule, it's better for one parent to tighten up a bit and for the other to loosen up a little to unify their approach to discipline. Otherwise, children may become confused by their parents' different philosophies or methodologies of child rearing. The second way that parents discipline inconsistently is by vacillating from day to day on either what is or what is not punishable behavior, and/or on how severe the chastisement will be. Children ought to know that their parents' "yes" means "yes" and that their "no" means "no." They should know that each offense will be treated justly and equitably regardless of their parents' emotional, spiritual, or physical condition at the time of discipline.

7. By Having Double Standards

> The things you have learned and received and heard and seen in me, practice these things; and the God of peace shall be with you. (Phil. 4:9)

The parent who uses the Bible to teach, reprove, correct, and instruct his children in righteousness, but is not willing to *practice* that same biblical righteousness in his own life, is not only a hypocrite but a provoker of his children. Have you ever heard your mother or father say, "Do as I say, not as I do"? Chances are, you haven't. This hypocritical message is communicated more often by actions (or lack of them) than by words. Regardless of how this message is communicated, when teenagers see their parents (their spiritual leaders) using double standards, this encourages their anger—much like the hypocrisy of the scribes and the Pharisees (the spiritual leaders of His day) angered Christ.

But before you start feeling too justified about your anger, let me remind you first of all that Christ didn't sin even when He was angry. Moreover, He was provoked by people much worse than your parents. The bottom line is that you are without excuse if you allow your parents' double standards to provoke you to a sinful response.

8. By Being Legalistic

The kind of legalism to which I'm referring is that which elevates man-made rules to the same level of culpability as God-given commands.

God has given each set of Christian parents the responsibility to develop from Scripture a biblically based economy or "law of the house" by which their children should abide. This collection of house rules contains two basic sections: *biblically directed rules* and *biblically derived rules*.

BIBLICALLY DIRECTED RULES *(which I will always be obligated to obey)*	BIBLICALLY DERIVED RULES *(which are based on biblical principles, but which I'm obligated to obey only as long as I'm under my parents' authority)*
Do not lie	Do not stay up past 9:00 p.m. on school nights
Do not covet	Do not leave the table without asking to be excused
Do not steal	Eat all of your broccoli

Your parents must develop ephemeral (short-lived) house rules in order to help establish and maintain order and unity in a household of sinners. Sometimes parents forget to make clear to their children the distinction between these man-made temporary rules and God's eternal ones. (Sometimes they don't know the difference between the two categories themselves.) I have seen this lack of distinction produce teens (and older adult children) who misunderstood, and consequently rejected, true Christianity because they believed it to be an antiquated, stale, rigid religion with no power to transform lives.

Christ often had to contend with this same kind of legalism from the religious leaders of His day. The scribes and the Pharisees held to and elevated the oral tradition (the Talmud) to such an extent that it became as legal and binding to some of them as the Scriptures. It may not have been wrong for them to follow their own man-made applications of Scripture (see Rom. 14:6), but when they imposed their man-made traditions on others, teaching these rules as though they were as obligatory as God's Law, they became bound up in legalism. It was to these leaders, who did not distinguish man-made from God-breathed commandments, that Christ, after calling them hypocrites, reiterated the words of Isaiah:

> This people honors Me with their lips,
> But their heart is far away from Me.
> But in vain do they worship Me,
> Teaching as doctrines the precepts of men. (Matt. 15:8–9)

Do you know the difference between these two categories of rules?

BIBLICALLY DIRECTED RULES (The Scripture)	BIBLICALLY DERIVED RULES (The Talmud)
Children obey your parents	Bedtime at 9:00 p.m. on school nights
You shall not steal	Eat all of your broccoli
Love the Lord	Make your bed every morning
Love your neighbor	Put dirty clothes in the hamper (not on the floor)
	Limited television
	Don't leave the table without asking to be excused

There is an important distinction that should be made between these two sections of "the law of the house." Whereas one may never appeal God's law, parental laws are appealable. The parent may not say dogmatically (without being legalistic), "It's God's will for *all* children *everywhere* to be in bed by 9:00 p.m. on school nights." However, they may say (if they are so inclined), "These are our house rules. If you would like to make a respectful appeal because of extenuating circumstances, we will consider it. When you are an adult, you will have your own house rules for your children. In the meantime, it's your responsibility to obey the house rules we established based on biblical principles. If you decide to let your children stay up past 9:00 p.m., we will not interfere or consider your decision to be wrong."

This is what you should always keep in mind: "The rules that my parents have established that are not clearly delineated in the Bible, I will be obligated to follow *only as long* as I'm under their authority." But, be they *biblically directed* (taken verbatim from the Bible) or *biblically derived* (based on biblical principles)—or, for that matter, based on little if any Scripture at all—as long as what your parents ask you to do is not a sin, you must obey. That's right; even if they don't have a clue about the biblical basis of their request, as long as their request is not a clear violation of God's Word, you will be in violation of Scripture if you *don't* obey (Eph. 6:1–2).

9. By Not Admitting When They Are Wrong

> If therefore you are presenting your offering at the altar, and there remember that your brother has something against you, leave your offering there before the altar, and go your way; first be reconciled to your brother, and then come and present your offering. (Matt. 5:23–24)

> Therefore, confess your sins to one another, and pray for one another. (James 5:16)

A parents' failure to acknowledge offenses committed against their children often discourages them from open biblical communication. When teens perceive such *insensitivity* and *pride* on the part of a parent, they often conclude, "It's no use trying to talk to him; he'll never admit to doing anything wrong." Of course, the criteria for such communication should not be whether or not Dad will hear, but rather whether or not Dad's sin is of such a nature that it cannot be overlooked (Prov. 19:11) or covered (Prov. 10:12; 17:9). In other words, teenagers should follow the advice beginning in Matthew 18:15 with their believing parents, regardless of the parental response.[2]

There is another passage in the Bible that gives instructions on what to do when someone has sinned against you and hasn't sought your forgiveness. These instructions, which we have already considered briefly in chapter 5 (Luke 17:3), are so important in helping teenagers to deal with the things that their believing parents do to provoke them to anger that I will explain them further in chapter 13.

10. By Constantly Finding Fault

> But the anger of Elihu . . . burned . . . against Job. . . . And his anger burned against his three friends, because they had found no answer, and yet had condemned Job. (Job 32:2–3)

What I'm concerned with here is not the parental responsibility to point out sinful behavior and character deficiencies in a child, but rather the critical, condemning, accusing, judgmental attitude that so often accompanies legitimate attempts at reproof. I'm referring to the kind of "spirit" that leads a teen to believe that his parents are never or rarely pleased with him.

When the Lord Jesus was reproving the Ephesian church for losing her first love, He began with a list of those behaviors that pleased Him (Rev. 2). I often tell parents, "Perhaps the most effective safeguard against this provocation is for you to purpose to praise, commend, and acknowledge biblical achievement with greater frequency than you reprove your children. This is not to imply a reduction in the number of reproofs, but rather to suggest an increase in the number of commendations."

If you believe your parents' "commendation to criticism ratio" is out of whack, maybe you should ask them to do a better job of balancing the good with the bad. Perhaps they would be willing to write out and discuss with you a list of both the positive and negative things about your character.

2. Although it deals with a different but somewhat parallel passage to Matthew 18:15ff, chapter 13 contains useful guidelines for helping teens to confront their sinning parents.

11. By Not Listening to the Teen's Opinion or "Side of the Story"

> He who gives an answer before he hears,
> It is folly and shame to him. (Prov. 18:13)

> The first to plead his case seems just,
> Until another comes and examines him. (Prov. 18:17)

Parents may not always agree with their teen's reasoning, conclusions, and opinions, but if they are going to lead him into the truth, they will need to understand his perspective. By not attempting to understand their teenager's perspective, parents often communicate such sinful attitudes as arrogance, impatience, apathy, or lack of love. People of all ages are inclined to translate rejection of their ideas as rejection of their persons. When there is a constant barrage of parental insensitivity in this area, teens quickly conclude (sometimes wrongly) that Mom and Dad, like the proverbial fool, are not interested in anything but their own opinions.

But you should learn how to receive reproof biblically without equating rejection of your ideas as personal rejection. If you have not yet checked out appendix B, in which I have outlined some of the common unbiblical responses to reproof as well as some guidelines for receiving reproof, you may want to do it now. Learning how to do this right just might motivate your parents to do a better job of listening to your concerns.

12. By Not Having Time to Talk

> Be quick to listen, slow to speak. (James 1:19 NIV)

> [There is] a time to be silent and a time to speak. (Eccl. 3:7 NIV)

Relationships are impossible to build apart from communication. As we have seen, to the degree that God has revealed Himself to us in the Bible, we may have a close relationship with Him. As parents and children alike reveal themselves to each other through various forms of communication, their relationship with each other is strengthened. Remember, revelation is a biblical prerequisite for effective relationships.

When Mom and Dad allow the pressures and pleasures of life to keep them from spending enough time in the revelation/communication process, strong parent/child relationships are not established. In addition to provoking children to wrath, this weakening of the parent/ child relationship motivates children to build closer relationships with friends than with parents. As a rule, your parents should be your closest (or at least among your closest) friends. Don't let your schedule keep you from spending time talking with them.

13. By Failing to Keep Promises

But let your statement be, "Yes, yes" or "No, no;" and anything beyond these is of evil. (Matt. 5:37)

[He] who keeps his oath
   even when it hurts
. . . .
will never be shaken. (Ps. 15:4–5 NIV)

Do not lie to one another, since you laid aside the old self with its evil practices. (Col. 3:9)

Promises and commitments are usually made with every intention of keeping them and with no intent to deceive. However, when promises and commitments consistently are not kept, regardless of the reason, and an attempt is not made to break the contract biblically (see Prov. 6:1–5) or forgiveness is not sought from a young person for breach of contract, disappointment often turns into anger. As the string of broken promises gets longer and longer and the teen increasingly views his parents as undependable, unreliable, and deceitful, his anger may intensify proportionately.

Many responses may occur in the heart of someone whose hopes have been dashed by broken promises. You may find yourself struggling with the following emotions unless you learn alternative biblical responses:

- Disappointment
- Suspicion (unwillingness to trust)
- Rejection (feeling hurt)
- Bitterness
- Thoughts of being unloved
- Loss of respect for your parents
- Contempt

Any of these, if not dealt with biblically, can easily lead to anger and then to rebellion.

14. By Giving Too Much Freedom

> The rod and reproof give wisdom,
> But a child who gets his own way brings shame to his mother.
> (Prov. 29:15)

Teens who grow up in homes with too much freedom and not enough discipline may quickly conclude that they are not truly loved by their parents. They understand, sometimes more than their parents do, the truth of Hebrews 12:6–9:

> "FOR THOSE WHOM THE LORD LOVES HE DISCIPLINES,
> AND HE SCOURGES EVERY SON WHOM HE RECEIVES."

> It is for discipline that you endure; God deals with you as with sons; for what son is there whom his father does not discipline? But if you are without discipline, of which all have become partakers, then you are illegitimate children and not sons. Furthermore, we had earthly fathers to discipline us, and we respected them; shall we not much rather be subject to the Father of spirits, and live?

There are at least four things that ought to limit the amount of freedom your parents give you:

1. The habitual practice of any sinful behavior
2. The lack of proficiency in the activities in which you want to participate. In other words, you have not yet demonstrated the appropriate levels of responsibility and maturity for the activity (e.g., having the freedom to dispose of great sums of money without knowing how to live by a biblically balanced budget)
3. The lack of self-control (don't be surprised if your parents limit your freedom because you live an undisciplined life, doing almost anything your heart desires, instantly gratifying every craving of your heart)
4. Unfaithfulness (not being dependable)—I will say more about this in the next point as well as in the final chapter of this book

15. By Not Giving Enough Freedom

The wisdom from above is first pure, then peaceable, gentle, reasonable [easy to be entreated], full of mercy. (James 3:17)

And from everyone who has been given much shall much be required; and to whom they entrusted much, of him they will ask all the more. (Luke 12:48)

Rather than expecting your parents to simply hand you freedom on a silver platter, you ought to be willing to earn freedom by showing them that you are faithful. Faithfulness involves demonstrating to God and to others that you can be trusted with more freedom based on at least two things: the successful fulfillment of specific responsibilities and the successive competence to make wise (biblical) decisions.

When teenagers demonstrate such faithfulness but parents do not reward them with the trust that is commensurate with (equal to) their achievement, they can become exasperated, discouraged, and even give up. Why is it that parents do not give their children enough freedom? Some of the reasons include insecurity, fear, unbiblical standards based on tradition rather than on Scripture, inordinate desires to have perfect children, and inordinate concern for what others might think.

Having said that, let me tell you that in my thirty years of counseling experience, I have rarely found parents who were not willing to cut loose with more freedom once their son or daughter demonstrated faithfulness. You are your parents' teacher. It's *you* who teaches them *by your level of maturity* how much freedom you deserve.

16. By Having Unrealistic Expectations

> When I was a child, I used to speak as a child, think as a child, reason as a child. (1 Cor. 13:11)

The Bible acknowledges that children think, speak, and reason differently from adults. The process whereby children grow and develop takes time. Additionally, one person may grow at a different rate than another.

Parents must take care to not impose standards and expectations on their children that their children are unable to perform developmentally unless those standards or expectations are clearly delineated in Scripture. Moreover, the emphasis should be on character, not on achievement. For example, godly character is shown in doing your best for God's glory, not necessarily in getting straight A's. Factored into the equation should also be the reality that all teens are sinners and are therefore going to sin. Hence it should not surprise parents when even obedient teenagers occasionally show their sinful hearts.

17. By Showing Favoritism toward One Child above Another

> Now his older son was in the field, and when he came and approached the house, he heard music and dancing. And he summoned one of the servants and began inquiring what these things might be. And he said to him, "Your brother has come, and your father has killed

the fattened calf, because he has received him back safe and sound."
But *he became angry*, and was not willing to go in; and his father came
out and began entreating him. But he answered and said to his father,
"Look! For so many years I have been serving you, and I have never
neglected a command of yours; and yet you have never given me a kid,
that I might be merry with my friends; but when this son of yours came,
who has devoured your wealth with harlots, you killed the fattened
calf for him." (Luke 15:25–30)

When the elder prodigal brother (wrongly) perceived that his
father was showing favoritism toward his younger prodigal brother,
the elder brother became angry. Siblings are different from each other
and therefore should be treated as individuals. The standard, however, by which each young person is evaluated and by which a parent
responds to each one should be identical (a point, by the way, that the
eldest prodigal brother did not understand, resulting in a misperception of his father's motive).

Think of a thermometer. When placed in a refrigerator, it may
read thirty-eight degrees Fahrenheit. When placed on the kitchen
table, it may read seventy-two degrees. When that same thermometer
is placed in an oven, it may read four hundred degrees. Did the thermometer ever change? Did it ever stop being a faithful instrument of
measuring the temperature? Did it ever stop becoming a thermometer
and become a wristwatch? Of course not! What changed is not the
thermometer, but rather its *environment* or *circumstance*. Likewise,
when you find that you're in a different set of circumstances from
your brother or sister, you want to have the assurance that you will
be treated similarly (with justice) by your parent to how your siblings would be treated if they found themselves in a similar set of
circumstances.

Now the question you may be asking is, "What am I supposed
do with this information?" Two things: one you can do right now; the
other I will tell you about in chapter 13 (there are a few more things I
must explain before giving you the second option). I have included a
Parental Provocation Worksheet (appendix C) for you to identify both

the things your folks do to "push your anger button" and how you typically respond. Take a moment right now (or at least before you begin the next chapter) to fill out this form. As you continue reading through this book, you will discover additional tools that will help you to learn more biblical responses to these provocations than the ones you are now using. Appendix C should prove to be a useful tool that will better enable you to understand and apply what lies ahead.

7

JOURNALING YOUR ANGER

HERE IS A TOOL that you can use to help you correct sinful manifestations of anger. When used correctly and consistently, the anger journal will help you to accomplish the following:

1. Identify the events that trigger your angry responses
2. Analyze and evaluate your inappropriate expressions of anger
3. Design alternative biblical responses to the events that trigger your anger
4. Improve your communication and conflict-resolution skills
5. Learn how to express anger without sinning

An anger journal is simply a sheet of paper on which, after each inappropriate expression of anger, you record the answers to four specific questions:

1. What happened that provoked me to anger? (What were the circumstances that led to my becoming angry?)
2. What did I say and/or do when I became angry? (How did I respond to the circumstances?)
3. What does the Bible say about what I said and/or did when I became angry? (What is the biblical terminology for what I said and/or did when I became angry?)
4. What should I have said and/or done when I became angry? (How could I have responded biblically when I became angry?)

ANGER JOURNAL

1. What happened that provoked me to anger? (What were the cir-
    cumstances that led to my becoming angry?)

    _____

    _____

    _____

    _____

    _____

    _____

    _____

2. What did I say and/or do when I became angry? (How did I respond
    to the circumstances?)

    _____

    _____

    _____

    _____

    _____

    _____

    _____

3. What does the Bible say about what I said and/or did when I became angry? (What is the biblical terminology for what I said and/or did when I became angry?)

_____

_____

_____

_____

_____

_____

_____

_____

4. What should I have said and/or done when I became angry? (How could I have responded biblically when I became angry?)

_____

_____

_____

_____

_____

_____

_____

_____

I have seen this simple four-step process help many people learn how to identify and correct sinful expressions of anger. If you are willing to invest some time and effort in learning how to do this, I know it can help you too.

Step One: Identify the circumstantial provocation of the anger.

QUESTIONS:

What happened that provoked me to anger?

or What were the circumstances that led to my becoming angry?

By identifying the external circumstance that triggers your internal anger response, you will accomplish two things. First, you will be better able to determine whether your anger is righteous or sinful. Let me emphasize again that not all anger is sinful. Note the following verses:

God is angry with the wicked every day. (Ps. 7:11 KJV)

[Jesus] looked round about on [the Pharisees] with anger. (Mark 3:5 KJV)

Be angry and do not sin. (Eph. 4:26 ESV)

If God is sometimes angry, if Jesus was sometimes angry, and if we as believers are commanded to be angry in certain circumstances, then to say that all anger is sinful is to accuse God of wrongdoing. God designed our bodies in such a way that during periods of stress, our adrenal glands secrete extra adrenaline. This is apparently the Creator's way of biologically energizing us (when angry) to do the right things in response to anger-producing circumstances.

I'm indebted to David Powlison of the Christian Counseling and Educational Foundation, who provided the idea for the following diagram. It's one of the best tools I know to help people determine whether or not their anger is sinful.

Righteous Anger	Sinful Anger
When God doesn't get what He wants	When I don't get what I want
God's will is violated	My will is violated
God is God	I am god

If your anger is due to your recognition that a holy God has been offended by another's behavior, that anger is righteous. In other words, if we are angry because God's revealed will (as found in the Bible) is violated (that is, if we are angry as a result of someone's sin), our anger is righteous.

On the other hand, if your anger is the result of not having your personal desires met, that anger is likely to be sinful. That is, if we are angry because someone (without violating Scripture) prevented us from having what we really wanted, our anger is sinful. Of course, it's possible (even probable in those situations where another person's sin against God is also an offense against us) to have both righteous anger and sinful anger residing in our hearts at the same time. By identifying circumstantial evidence, it's often possible to preliminarily distinguish righteous anger from sinful anger.

The second benefit of identifying the circumstantial triggers to anger has to do with recognizing habitual response patterns. You may find that certain kinds of events trigger your angry response. Maybe there is one (or several common denominators) that, like a wrongly colored thread, runs through the entire fabric of your anger-provoking circumstances.

For example, I discovered several years ago that in my own life, much of what angered (frustrated) me involved *time* and *money*. This insight helped me to recognize the extent to which I was both a "lover of money" (see 2 Tim. 3:2) and a "lover of pleasure" (see 2 Tim. 3:4). To the degree that I would become sinfully angry when someone messed with (what I thought was) my money, I loved money more than God. The fact that when my "spare time" was threatened I became angry—time when I would normally enjoy pleasures such as fishing or hunting—indicated that I loved my diversionary activities too much.

As a review of the circumstantial anger triggers in my own life revealed a tendency to become angry over things that pertain to time and money, so a review of your anger journal may reveal those things in your life that tend to trigger anger most often. These "hot buttons" that you discover can serve to help you identify those things that you have idolized (lusted after to the point of idolatry) in your heart.

Righteous Anger	Sinful Anger
When God doesn't get what He wants	When I don't get what I want
God's will is violated	My will is violated
Motivation: Sincere love for God	Motivation: Love of my heart's idol
Christ is Lord of my life	I am lord (boss) of my life

Pause and consider those things that tend to push your "hot button" to see if you can put your finger on what might be common denominators of provocation to sinful anger. As I said, we will delve further into the issue of motive shortly.

Step Two: Describe the outward manifestations of the anger.

QUESTIONS:

What did I say and/or do when I became angry?

or How did I respond to the circumstances?

By specifying the details of an angry response, you can see your words and actions in black and white. This exercise, in addition to being a prerequisite for a biblical diagnosis of whether or not your response was sinful, aids you in remembering different elements of a compound response. That is, it can help you break down your response into bite-sized pieces for a more thorough examination.

Record your verbal responses verbatim (excluding any vulgarities and profanities). Carefully note your tone of voice and nonverbal language. Vindictive actions such as slamming doors, hitting or throwing objects, physical assaults, and other retaliatory measures you took should be recorded as well.

Step Three: Evaluate biblically the exact nature of the anger.

QUESTIONS:

What does the Bible say about what I said and/or did when I became angry?

or What is the biblical terminology for what I said and/or did when I became angry?

A problem cannot be solved biblically until it is diagnosed using biblical terminology. Only then can you know where to look in Scripture for insights and direction on how to change. Only then can you choose the biblical alternatives to be put on in place of those to be put off. Usually it's not enough just to say, "I was sinfully angry." The manifestations of sinful anger are identified in the Bible with much greater specificity than that. The following chart may be helpful in assisting you in your evaluation. It pinpoints some common manifestations of anger using precise biblical terminology. I have subdivided this chart into two classifications of observable behavior: actions (and attitudes) and words.

Let me recommend that you look up and discuss each biblical reference to fully understand the meaning of each term as a part of your daily Bible or quiet time. The more readily you can identify specific manifestations of anger, the easier it will be for you to recognize such manifestations, not only in your life but also in the lives of others.

Actions (and Attitudes)	Words
Vengeance (Rom. 12)	Disrespectful (1 Tim. 6:2)
Striker (1 Tim. 3:3)	Sarcastic (Neh. 4:3)
Hateful (Gal. 5:20)	Name-calling (Eph. 4:29)
Unkind (Eph. 4:32)	Cursing (Col. 3:8)
Unloving (1 Cor. 13)	Gossip (Prov. 11:13)
Bitter (Heb. 12:15)	Clamor (Eph. 4:31)
Wrath (Eph. 4:31)	Biting/Devouring (Eph. 5:15)
Uncontrolled (Rom. 1:31; 2 Tim. 3:13)	Emulations (Gal. 5:19)
Hurtful (Eph. 4:31–32)	Strife (Gal. 5:20)
Malice (Rom. 1:29; Eph. 4:31)	Debate (Rom. 1:29)
Variance (Gal. 5:20)	Delight (Rom. 1:29)
Despiteful (Rom. 1:30)	Whispering (Rom. 1:29)
Pride (Rom. 1:30)	Backbiting (Rom. 1:30)
Disobedient (Rom. 1:30)	Boasting (Rom. 1:30)
Unforgiving (Luke 17)	Blaspheme (2 Tim. 3:2)
Unmerciful (Rom. 1:31)	False accusation (2 Tim. 3:3)
Impatience (Eph. 4:2)	Scorning and Mocking
Intolerance (Eph. 4:2)	Grumbling/Complaining (Phil 2:14)
Ungrateful (2 Tim. 3:2)	Vulgarity (Col. 3:8)
Selfishness (Mark 7:22; 1 Cor. 13)	Grievous words (Prov. 15:11)
Falsely Accusing (Prov. 14:5)	
Quarrelsome (1 Tim. 3:3)	

Step Four: Develop an alternative biblical response to the circumstantial provocation.

QUESTIONS:

What should I have said and/or done when I became angry?

or How could I have responded biblically when I became angry?

This is perhaps the most important step. It's the step where you can make use of the Scriptures for *correction* and *disciplined training in righteousness* (2 Tim. 3:16). As you prayerfully consider various alternative biblical responses to the ones you originally chose, you not only demonstrate repentance (a change of mind), but you also prepare yourself for future provocations (temptations) by exercising yourself for the purpose of godliness (1 Tim. 4:7).

It's important for you to keep in mind that there is usually any number of biblically acceptable responses. I recommend that you develop at least two or three alternatives for each wrong response you have recorded under step two. The more time you spend pondering potential answers, the greater your exercise in righteousness will be. "The heart of the righteous ponders how to answer" (Prov. 15:28). The more time you spend in this step of the journal, the wiser (and gentler) you will become. "The heart of the righteous teaches his mouth, and adds persuasiveness to his lips" (Prov. 16:23).

Perhaps by now, based on what I have said previously, you have anticipated what comes next: namely, that each part of the anger journal is to be reviewed with a parent, mature friend, or counselor. Having written out two or three alternative responses, you may even want to rehearse each biblical response (through each part of what we called the "communication pie") until you have it honed to precision.

APPLICATIONS OF THE ANGER JOURNAL

The anger journal may be used in virtually any circumstance in which you become angry. The pages that follow contain some examples.

ANGER JOURNAL

1. What happened that provoked me to anger? (What were the circumstances that led to my becoming angry?)

   When I asked Mom if she would buy a paint gun for me that was on sale at Walmart, she said, "No." She said that the last time she bought me one, I used it to shoot at my little brother and the family pets when I got mad at them.

2. What did I say and/or do when I became angry? (How did I respond to the circumstances?)

   I raised my voice and said, "That's not fair! You never buy me anything. Dad would have bought it for me." I then ran out to the car and left her to carry all the packages by herself.

3. What does the Bible say about what I said and/or did when I became angry? (What is the biblical terminology for what I said and/or did when I became angry?)

   Not a soft answer/grievous wounds (Prov. 15:1); Argumentative (2 Tim. 2:24); Murmuring/complaining (Phil. 2:14); False accusation / lying (Eph. 4:25); Disrespectful (Eph. 6:1–3); Vindictive (Rom. 12:17–21); Malicious (Eph. 4:31); Unloving, unkind, bad manners (1 Cor. 13)

4. What should I have said and/or done when I became angry? (How could I have responded biblically when I became angry?)

   I should have said, "Yes, Mom." I should have said, "I don't blame you for not trusting me. I'm going to work extra hard to show you that I can be trusted with a paint gun." I should have offered to carry the packages to the car for her.

ANGER JOURNAL

1. What happened that provoked me to anger? (What were the circumstances that led to my becoming angry?)

   I was shooting baskets in our driveway when my dad stuck his head out the back door and insisted that I come in to begin doing my homework. He told my friend who was shooting with me to come back tomorrow.

2. What did I say and/or do when I became angry? (How did I respond to the circumstances?)

   "I don't have any homework, and you're always running my friends off. It's no wonder they all think you and Mom are idiots." Then I cussed at him under my breath (but loud enough so that my friend could hear me), slammed the basketball into the back door (breaking the window), and stomped off to my room, sulking and pouting as I went.

3. What does the Bible say about what I said and/or did when I became angry? (What is the biblical terminology for what I said and/or did when I became angry?)

   Lying (I did have homework, and my friends don't all think my parents are idiots), profanity, slander, backbiting, hate, having a sad countenance.

4. What should I have said and/or done when I became angry? (How could I have responded biblically when I became angry?)

   Said, "OK, Dad" and explained to my friend that I really did have homework to do but that, if I finished it early, I'd give him a call. Made an appeal: "Dad, I have some new information. May I make an appeal?" (Yes) "One of my teachers was out sick today, and the substitute teacher allowed us to catch up on some homework, so I only have to study for two subjects instead of my usual four. In light of this, may I stay out and shoot baskets for another 45 minutes?" I could have made an appeal to my father about adjusting my schedule when it doesn't leave time for playing basketball. Appeal to Dad to buy lights for the driveway so I can play basketball after dark (provided I get my homework done). "How about it, Dad?!"

ANGER JOURNAL

1. What happened that provoked me to anger? (What were the circumstances that led to my becoming angry?)

   I was invited to a sleepover with four of my friends. When I asked if I could go, my parents said "no." I tried to appeal (before I heard their reasons for saying no), but they wouldn't let me.

2. What did I say and/or do when I became angry? (How did I respond to the circumstances?)

   I gave them a loud sigh, rolled my eyes at them in disgust, stomped off to my room and slammed the door (very loudly).

3. What does the Bible say about what I said and/or did when I became angry? (What is the biblical terminology for what I said and/or did when I became angry?)

   I was disrespectful (Ex. 20:12; Prov. 1:8–9). I was disobedient (Rom. 13:1–6; Eph. 6:1–4). I was proud (Prov. 16:5; 18:3; Isa. 2:10–22). I was quick to anger over not getting what I wanted (Eccl. 7:9; Eph. 4:26; James 1:19; 4:1–4). I was harboring bitterness in my heart (Heb. 12:15; James 3:13–18). I "answered a matter before I heard it" (Prov. 18:2, 13, 17).

4. What should I have said and/or done when I became angry? (How could I have responded biblically when I became angry?)

   I should have heard my parents out thoroughly before I attempted to make an appeal. If my appeal was rejected, I should have taken it as from the Lord (assumed He didn't want me to go) and addressed my parents respectfully.

ANGER JOURNAL

1. What happened that provoked me to anger? (What were the circumstances that led to my becoming angry?)

   The youth group at our church was going to see a movie on Saturday evening. The movie was to end later than my normal curfew. When I asked if I could go, my parents said they'd talk about it. The answer was "no" because Dad wanted to make sure my heart (and my body) was ready for church on Sunday morning.

2. What did I say and/or do when I became angry? (How did I respond to the circumstances?)

   "Yes sir," I answered politely. But in my heart, I was resentful, angry, and bitter. I sulked in my heart all night long.

3. What does the Bible say about what I said and/or did when I became angry? (What is the biblical terminology for what I said and/or did when I became angry?)

   I was sinfully angry (Eph. 4:26; James 1:19–20). I was proud (Mic. 6:6–8; Col. 3:12–17). I was harboring hatred in my heart (John 13:34–35; 1 Cor. 13). I was giving in to self-pity (1 Kings 19:19; Phil. 2:14).

4. What should I have said and/or done when I became angry? (How could I have responded biblically when I became angry?)

   I should have trusted my parents' judgment and believed that God was going to work this disappointment out for my good (Rom. 8:28–29). Instead of sulking in my room, I could have put my mind to better use (like figuring out how to do something nice for my parents who love me enough to give me what I need—and for the most part, what I want).

"I'm sure this is a very helpful tool, but the anger journal seems to deal only with external responses. What about helping me to change my thoughts and motives? Shouldn't these things be addressed as well?"

I'm glad you asked. Yes, they certainly should be addressed. In the chapters that follow, I will give you instructions that will help you to identify and change wrong thoughts and motives and replace them with appropriate biblical alternatives.

8

GETTING TO THE HEART OF ANGER, PART 1

LET'S DO AN EXPERIMENT. I'm going to ask you to attempt to emote on command. I will ask you to generate an emotion in your heart with which you are probably well acquainted. Are you ready? Good! Sit up straight in your chair, take a deep breath, and let it out slowly. Good! Now take another breath and let it out slowly. Very good! OK, here we go.

One, two, three . . . *hate!* That's right! *Hate me!* Come on; you can do it! Hate! Hate! Hate!

What's wrong? Some of you are smiling; others are chuckling. You are supposed to be hating.

"But, Lou, it's not easy to whip up a good hate. It just won't whip."

That's right! Most of you are having great difficulty feeling hatred for a person who has done you no wrong. Had I done something to hurt you, or had you perceived that I had done so, it would have been a different story. You might have thought, "That Priolo dude! How could he do such a thing! Doesn't he realize how wrong it was to treat me that way! He wouldn't like it if someone had done that to him. That's what I'll do. I'll do it back to him. Maybe then he'll understand how much it hurt."

If you think such thoughts, you will probably find it much easier to hate. Why is that? It's because, as we have seen, our feelings are largely the by-products of our thoughts and actions. (If you had turned your vengeful thoughts into vengeful actions, the hatred would likely have flowed even more freely). By the way, if you do not have much difficulty hating on command, may I suggest that it's because you already have an inordinate amount of hatred in your heart for (or bitterness toward) someone, and thus have the ability to transfer such hatred to any other person with relative ease.

In chapter 5, you learned how to identify and conquer your *external* manifestations of sinful anger. In this chapter and the next, you will learn how to identify and conquer *internal* manifestations of sinful anger. These two chapters, although rather technical in nature, may very well be the most important for you because they deal with the root of the problem—your sinful heart.

WHAT IS THE HEART?

In his *Theology of Christian Counseling*, Dr. Jay E. Adams calls the human heart "the source or treasure-house from which the outer words and actions spring." He explains,

> In order to help us better understand the biblical meaning of heart, let us ask, "What, then, is set over against heart, if anything?" The answer is *always*, without exception, *the visible outer man*. Worship that one gives with his *lips* (outer, visible, audible worship) when his *heart* (inner, invisible, inaudible) is far from God is a good example of this contrast (Matt. 15:8). We are instructed that man looks on the "*outward appearance*" but (in contrast) "God looks on the *heart*" (1 Sam. 16:7). Without multiplying references, it is safe to say that everywhere the Bible uses the word *heart* to speak of the inner man (or, as Peter puts it in a thoroughly definitive way, "the hidden person of the heart"). Plainly, then, heart in the Bible is the inner life that one lives before God and himself, a life that is unknown by others because it is hidden from them.[1]

Do you remember our analogy of the inner man (heart) and the outer man (lips, mouth, tongue, and so on) that I made in chapter 3? Let me expand on it for a moment.

1. Jay E. Adams, *A Theology of Christian Counseling* (Grand Rapids: Zondervan, 1979), 114–15.

The reservoir part of the pitcher that holds the liquid is analogous to your heart. The spout of the pitcher is like your mouth (or tongue, lips, countenance, etc.). Whatever substance is contained in the reservoir will pour out of the spout when the pitcher is appropriately tilted.

If the pitcher were filled with milk, what would pour out of the spout?

If the pitcher were filled with iced tea, what would pour out of the spout?

If the pitcher were filled with nail polish remover, what would pour out of the spout?

If your heart is filled with foolishness, what will pour out of your mouth (Prov. 12:23; 15:2)?

If your heart is filled with deceit, what will pour out of your mouth (Prov. 12:20)?

If your heart is filled with pride, what will pour out of your mouth (Pss. 101:5; 131:1)?

If your heart is filled with anger, what will pour out of your mouth (Prov. 26:24–26)?

If your heart is filled with wisdom, what will flow out of your mouth (Col. 3:16)?

If your heart is filled with virtue, what will flow out of your mouth (Prov. 22:11)?

And if your heart is filled with gentleness (an antidote to sinful anger), what will flow out of your mouth (1 Peter 3:4)?

Unlike the contents of the pitcher in the above illustration, man cannot see what is in the hearts of others. Only God knows for sure what is inside. Your parents, siblings, and friends can get a glimpse into your heart only by observing what pours out into your words, actions, and attitudes.

"The mouth speaks out of that which fills the heart. The good man out of his good treasure brings forth what is good; and the evil man out of his evil treasure brings forth what is evil" (Matt. 12:34–35). Perhaps this is why James said, "No one can tame the tongue; it is a restless evil and full of deadly poison" (James 3:8). The tongue is just a muscle that does what it's told to do by the heart. The tongue cannot be brought under control by a heart that is out of control. "If you have bitter jealousy and selfish ambition" (v. 14) in your heart, what may ultimately be said by your tongue will be cursing (vv. 9–10), commotion, and every evil thing (v. 16).

Your believing parents have been commanded to bring you up in the discipline and admonition of the Lord (Eph. 6:4). They have probably tried in a variety of ways to drive out the foolishness that was (and perhaps still is) "bound up" in your heart (Prov. 22:15) and to help you replace it with the wisdom of Scripture. "The *heart* of the wise teaches his *mouth*, and adds persuasiveness to his *lips*" (Prov. 16:23). Notice once again the contrast between the heart and the mouth.

Remember that although Scripture forbids us from judging what is in the heart of another (1 Cor. 4:5; James 2:4), we are permitted to ask others to judge their own thoughts and motives (Acts 5:1–4; 1 Cor. 11:28–31; 2 Cor. 13:5). Consider Proverbs 20:5: "The purposes of a man's heart are deep waters, but a man of understanding draws them out" (NIV).

By asking you specific questions, your believing parents can and should draw out of your heart the necessary information they must have to help you to biblically diagnose any sin problem that resides therein. To the extent that they can draw the counsel out of your heart, they will be able to help you to change not only your words, actions, and attitudes, but also (and more importantly) your thoughts and motives. And this is the "heart of the matter" when it comes to helping anyone to change. To the extent that they are not able to draw out the thoughts and motives of your heart, their ability to help you to change at the deepest level (the only kind of change that pleases God) will be hindered. This is why it's so essential for you to open up to your parents and to give them the information they need to have to bring you up properly. For you not to give them the information they need to bring you up "in the discipline and instruction of the Lord" (Eph. 6:4) is to hinder them from obeying God.

Of course, the Scriptures are needed for proper evaluation of one's heart: "For the word of God is living and active and sharper than any two-edged sword, and piercing as far as the division of soul and spirit, of both joints and marrow, and *able to judge the thoughts and intentions of the heart*" (Heb. 4:12). This is the only divinely approved diagnostic manual whereby Christians may accurately judge thoughts and motives. If your parents are Christians, they have a biblical responsibility not only to draw the thoughts and motives out of your heart but also to know how to diagnose those thoughts and motives "not in words taught by human wisdom, but in those taught by the Spirit, combining [interpreting] spiritual thoughts with spiritual words" (1 Cor. 2:13).

The goal of their training and discipline is to develop within you the character of Christ. In Romans 12:2, Paul explains that a Christian is totally transformed by the renewing of his mind. The process whereby this spiritual metamorphosis occurs takes place largely beneath the surface—in the heart of each believer. Your Christian parents have not done enough if they simply teach you how to behave like a Christian. As I have said, it's their responsibility to teach you how to *think* and *be motivated* like a Christian, for only then can change in your behavior be efficacious (effective) to the glory of God.

THE HEART JOURNAL

However, this book is written not for your parents, but for you. You are no longer a little child but rather an *emerging* adult. Now you must take an increasing measure of responsibility for correcting those things in your life that are not pleasing to God. Regardless of the level of help that your parents give you, God expects you to learn to "take every thought captive" (see 2 Cor. 10:5), to speak the truth in your heart (see Ps. 15:2), and to "be transformed by the renewing of your mind" (Rom. 12:2). So I would like to introduce you to a biblically derived approach that will ultimately help you to identify and correct sinful anger before it ever has a chance to bleed out of your mouth or onto your face.

Like the Anger Journal, the Heart Journal is a worksheet on which you record the answers to four specific questions after each angry response. The Heart Journal is a tool you can use to identify unbiblical *thoughts* and *motives* associated with your sinful anger. It's a worksheet on which you can record the answers to four sets of self-examination questions after your anger manifests itself.

1. What happened that provoked me to anger? (What were the circumstances that led to my becoming angry?)
2. What did I say to myself (in my heart) when I became angry? (What did I want, desire, or long for when I became angry?)
3. What does the Bible say about what I said to myself when I became angry? (What does the Bible say about what I wanted when I became angry?)
4. What should I have said to myself when I became angry? (What should I have wanted more than my own selfish/idolatrous desires?)

HEART JOURNAL

1. What happened that provoked me to anger? (What were the circumstances that led to my becoming angry?)

_____

_____

_____

_____

_____

_____

_____

2. What did I say to myself (in my heart) when I became angry? (What did I want, desire, or long for when I became angry?)

_____

_____

_____

_____

_____

_____

_____

3. What does the Bible say about what I said to myself when I became angry? (What does the Bible say about what I wanted when I became angry?)

_____

_____

_____

_____

_____

_____

_____

4. What should I have said to myself when I became angry? (What should I have wanted more than my own selfish/idolatrous desires?)

_____

_____

_____

_____

_____

_____

_____

The Heart Journal is especially helpful in identifying and correcting the sinful anger that resides within. By using the Heart Journal regularly, you can train yourself to do several things:

1. Distinguish between sinful anger and righteous anger in your heart
2. Identify your sinful thoughts and motives
3. Repent of (change) the unbiblical thoughts and motives associated with your sinful anger
4. Replace sinful thoughts and motives with those that are "true, honest, just, and pure" (see Phil. 4:8 KJV)

And, when used in conjunction with the Anger Journal,

5. Prevent your righteous anger from coming across as sinful anger

There is nothing magical about the wording of these journals. You may adjust the terminology of the Heart Journal (and Anger Journal) to your liking, provided that the basic concepts of each step are not altered.

Step One: Identify the circumstantial provocation of the anger.

QUESTIONS:

What happened that provoked me to anger?

or What were the circumstances that led to my becoming angry?

As you can see, the first question for the Heart Journal is identical to the first question for the Anger Journal and for pretty much the same reasons. First, the answer to this question helps to determine whether your anger is righteous or sinful. Second, it identifies any habit patterns associated with the events that tend to trigger anger. This answer, in turn, will make it easier to recognize and eventually dethrone any idolatrous desires which, when worshipped (coveted after), produce sinful anger.

The answer to these questions (only one answer is required here because both questions are really asking for the same information) will

123

make it easier to identify the circumstances in which you are most prone to be tempted. By comparing them to the first answers of your other journal entries, you may see a pattern of temptation to anger developing.

Step Two: Identify specific motives and thoughts associated with the anger.

QUESTIONS:

What did I say to myself (in my heart) when I became angry?

and What did I want, desire, or long for when I became angry?

Notice, first of all, that unlike the Anger Journal, the two questions in this step are separated not by the word or but rather by the word and. This is because all sets of questions in the Anger Journal are paraphrases of each other while the remaining sets of questions in the Heart Journal are not. The questions are similar but are not synonymous. Both questions in each set must be answered, because each question is addressing a different issue of the heart. The first question of each set focuses on the thoughts of the heart. The second question focuses on the motives of the heart.

Our ability to discern thoughts and motives when experiencing intense emotion is an essential skill for Christians who want to please God. Recognizing thoughts and imaginations of the heart is a prerequisite of bringing them "captive to the obedience of Christ" (2 Cor. 10:5; see also Deut. 15:9; Ps. 15:2; Isa. 55:7; Jer. 4:14; Matt. 15:19). But our ability to recognize our own sinful thoughts and motives is made more difficult due to the following factors:

1. "The heart is deceitful above all things" (Jer. 17:9 NKJV) and cannot be "known" apart from the Word of God, which is able to discern its thoughts and motives (see Heb. 4:12).
2. The heart's voice is often camouflaged by its own desires. That is, it's hard to detect wrong thoughts because they are often based on desires that may seem legitimate when, in fact, they are either wrong desires or legitimate desires that are desired inordinately (James 1:12–16; 4:1–2).

3. The heart has the capacity to speak to itself at the rate of over 1300 words per minute (especially when anger is triggering our adrenal glands to pump extra adrenaline into our systems), making such detection a bit complicated.

In answer to the first question of step two, "What did I say to myself (in my heart) when I became angry?", you should write out verbatim the thoughts that go through your mind at the moment of provocation. Such thoughts typically involve frequent first-person references (I, me, mine, and so on), so write down your thoughts that way ("I hate it when she looks at me that way!"). At first, you may be able to recognize only one or two sentences. In time and with practice you may be able to list a half dozen or more. Here are a few examples of the kind of responses for which I'm looking.

- "That's not fair!"
- "I don't have time for this."
- "I hate it when . . ."
- "I'll show her . . ."
- "She can't make me do that!"
- "I'm not going to do it."
- "Why doesn't she just _____?"
- "I want it, and I'm going to have it!"
- "She is such a _____."
- "He doesn't love me."
- "I can't wait till I can leave this place."
- "My parents are slave drivers."
- "They never let me have any fun."
- "I don't like it when . . ."
- "Here he goes again: lecture number 57."

Before moving on, I'd like to ask you another question. In what do you delight? Or, to ask the same question in another way, In what do you "seek your happiness"?

"Seek your happiness in the LORD, and He will give you your heart's desire" (Ps. 37:4 GNT). God has given us the ability to delight in anything we choose. We may delight in another person, a job, a particular sporting activity, a hobby, an automobile, a particular style of dress, travel—anything on which we set our hearts. But is it wrong to delight in any of these things? It's wrong if the object of such delighting is more of a delight than the Lord is. To put it another way, if the object of our delight is focused on anything other than God, the object of delight is likely an idol. Consider the following diagrams.

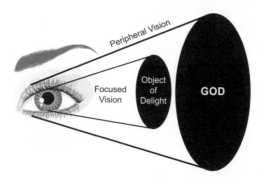

If we focus our delight on the objects themselves, seeing God only with our peripheral vision if at all, then our focus is wrong. If, on the other hand, we can see our objects of delight with our peripheral vision, all the while focusing on the gracious God who richly gives us all things to enjoy, and if we can use those objects as means to praise our Creator, then we are worshiping God in our hearts rather than worshiping our idolatrous desires.

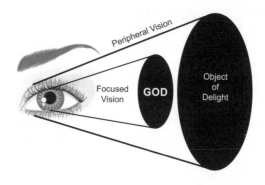

The answer to the second question of step two, "What did I want, desire, or long for when I became angry?", may be a bit more difficult to determine. Motives (passions, desires, affections, and so on) are not always as readily available to awareness as thoughts are. It's often not until you stop and ask yourself specific questions concerning these things that you can put your finger on what they are. If you have difficulty identifying your motives by asking yourself this question on the Heart Journal, try some of these questions:

1. What is it that I believe I can't be happy without?
2. What is it that I crave?
3. What is it that I believe I must have?
4. What do I spend most of my spare time thinking about?
5. What is it that I worry most about losing?
6. What is it in which I delight (seek my happiness) the most?
7. What is it that I love more than I love God and my neighbor?

When introducing the Heart Journal to a new counselee at our counseling center, I typically have him answer only the first two sets of questions on his own. Then I show him how to answer questions three and four in the following counseling session. You may want to follow a similar pattern, writing out the answers to questions one and two on your own, then asking your folks or one of your church leaders to help you to answer questions three and four (or at least letting them review your answer for a while until you get the hang of it).

Another option is for you to answer questions one and two as soon as (or soon after) you are provoked. Then, sometime later that day (or perhaps as a part of your quiet time the following day), answer questions three and four when you can devote more time to the project.

Here are some common teenage desires that you may want to consider as you answer this question. Those on the left are desires that are inherently wrong. Those on the right are desires that, although not inherently wrong, may be desired too intensely.

Unlawful Desires	Lawful Desires
I wanted to control (manipulate) my parents.	I wanted to play.
I wanted to get even.	I wanted to stay up late.
I wanted to be praised.	I wanted to do what I wanted.
I wanted something that belonged to another.	I wanted to be loved.
I wanted to hurt or murder someone.	I wanted a new gadget.
	I wanted more freedom.
	I wanted to go out.
	I wanted to go fishing.
	I wanted to have fun.

If you are going to identify and dethrone any of the idolatrous desires (idols) in your heart, you must first be certain that you can distinguish those desires that are sinful in and of themselves from those desires that are not. Of course this means that you will have to become more familiar with certain Scripture passages than you probably are. Appendix D, "Idolatrous 'Loves' in the Bible," has been included to assist you in this matter. In the next chapter I will explain how to answer questions three and four of the Heart Journal.

9

GETTING TO THE HEART OF ANGER, PART 2

ONE THING CANNOT be overemphasized: a problem cannot be solved biblically until it's diagnosed using biblical terminology. Only then can you know where to look in the Scriptures for insights and direction for change. Only then can you identify the biblical alternatives that are to be put on in place of those that are to be put off.

Learning how to identify the thoughts and motives of your heart and to evaluate them according to Scripture (Heb. 4:12) is foundational to bringing them "captive to the obedience of Christ" (2 Cor. 10:5). As we've already learned, the diagnosis should be made "not in words taught us by human wisdom but in words taught by the Spirit, expressing [interpreting] spiritual truths in spiritual words" (1 Cor. 2:13 NIV). The practice of familiarizing yourself with the terminology of Scripture combined with the exercise of writing down the appropriate diagnosis should, over time, build biblical discernment into your heart as you develop a mature conscience. "But solid food is for the mature, who because of practice have their senses trained to discern good and evil" (Heb. 5:14).

The third and fourth steps of the Heart Journal are practical exercises to help you discern between good and evil. This is the sign of a mature (grown-up) believer.

Step Three: Evaluate biblically the exact nature of the anger-producing thoughts and motives.

QUESTIONS:

What does the Bible say about what I said to myself when I became angry?

and What does the Bible say about what I wanted when I became angry?

When you are answering the question, "What does the Bible teach about what I said in my heart when I became angry?", think in terms of identifying specific categories of sin (e.g., pride, selfishness, hatred, malice, bitterness, and so on)—unless, of course, your thoughts were not sinful.

Let us say, for example, that in response to your parents' having forbidden you to visit with a close friend due to a prior commitment they had made that involves you, your thoughts may be as follows:

That's not fair.
My mother never lets me do what I want to do.
She doesn't want me to have any fun.
She is afraid that I'll get into trouble.
She's an obsessive, overbearing terrorist.
I can't wait to get out of here.

Using the Heart Journal, you would then evaluate each thought by using the biblical terminology that best describes the sins associated with the thought.

That's not fair.
- *False accusation / bad theology.* Even God is not "fair"; He is just. My mother has not been unjust in her dealing with me (Phil. 4:8; 2 Tim. 3:2–3). (For those of you who decide to do this during your quiet time, let me encourage you to use your concordance to find appropriate Scripture references that can be cited after each evaluation.)

- *Irresponsibility/selfishness.* I should be more concerned about keeping my promises than having fun (Ps. 15:4).

My mother never lets me do what I want to do.
- *Dishonesty.* She doesn't always keep me from doing what I want to do (Phil. 4:8).
- *Selfishness.* What I wanted to do is not as important as honoring my mother (1 Cor. 13:5; Eph. 6:2).

She doesn't want me to have any fun.
- *Judging motives.* I don't know what she wants because I cannot read her mind, and she has not told me what she wants (1 Cor. 4:5).
- *Being unloving.* Love believes that which is best about another. I should therefore put the best possible interpretation on her actions (1 Cor. 13:7).

She's an obsessive, overbearing terrorist.
- *False accusation / dishonesty.* It's certainly possible that her motives are unselfish and that she has what she believes is a good reason to keep me from seeing my friend.
- *Name calling / evil speaking.* There is not enough evidence to convict her of being obsessive or overbearing. A terrorist is not a name that God uses to classify people, and therefore I should probably not use it (1 Cor. 2:13; James 4:11).

I can't wait to get out of here.
- *Impatience.* The Lord has placed me in this family for His purposes. It's for Him to decide when I leave (Eph. 4:2).
- *Ungratefulness.* I should be focusing on what my parents have already given me rather than on what I wish they would give me (1 Thess. 5:18).

The second question in step three, "What does the Bible say about what I wanted when I became angry?", is used to evaluate (classify) your motives as either wrong or right.

If the desire is in and of itself a sin, the evaluation is relatively simple.

Motive	Biblical Evaluation
I wanted to get even.	Revenge
I wanted to look at pornography.	Lust
I wanted to kill him.	Murder
I wanted to trick him.	Deception
I did not want to obey my parents.	Disobedience
I did not want to share my things.	Selfishness

If, however, the desire is not inherently sinful, the question then becomes, "Did I want too *much* of something that God says is good, or did I want some good thing so much that I was willing either to sin *in order to get it* (by getting angry) or to sin *because I couldn't have it* (again by getting angry)?"

The book of James was possibly the first New Testament book to be written. The Christians to whom the Lord's brother was writing were having such conflicts with each other that James used the words *wars* and *fightings* (battles) to describe the outward manifestation of their anger. In the beginning of chapter four, the question he asks cuts right through such outward manifestations and focuses on the internal causes or motives of the anger. "What is the *source* of quarrels [wars] and conflicts [fightings] among you?" (James 4:1). He then answers his own question to reveal to the readers exactly what is at the heart of their angry disputes, or what is *in* their hearts that produced their angry disputes: "Is not the source [of these quarrels and conflicts] the *pleasures* that wage war in your members?" "Yes" is the intended reply.

We have angry conflicts with one another because our pleasures (desires which are not necessarily sinful in and of themselves) have become so intense that they are at war within our members. One of the military strategies that soldiers sometimes use is to hide out by digging into the ground and waiting for the enemy to arrive. (There is an Old Testament Hebrew term for waging war that has as its root the idea of being "encamped.") When our desires (as good as they may be) become so strong that they "camp out" in (or dig themselves deeply into) our hearts, those desires (as good as they may be) become sinful, idolatrous desires—not because they are sinful desires per se, but because they are desired *inordinately*. Our hearts covet them so intensely that we are willing to sin (war and fight) either *in order* to obtain them or because we are *not able* to obtain them.

James, in chapter four, continues to focus on the Christians' motives by unpacking in more detail what he has just said. "You lust [a different word that also implies a desire for something that is not inherently sinful] and do not have so you commit murder [a biblical effigy for and manifestation of hatred; see Matt. 5:21–22; 1 John 3:15]. And you are envious [another synonym for desire, with an implication of coveting which is sometimes associated with anger; see Acts 7:9; 17:5] and cannot obtain: so you fight and quarrel [verbal forms of the words *fightings* and *quarrels* in verse one, which mean 'to strive or dispute' and 'to contend or quarrel' respectively]" (v. 2).

After unpacking verse one (breaking it down into its component parts), James continues to press home his point that the cause of their relationship problems is their selfish, idolatrous motives, as evidenced by their self-centered prayer life.

> You do not have because you do not ask. You ask and do not receive, because you ask with wrong motives, so that you may spend it on your pleasures [the same word for *pleasure* that was used in verse one, from which our English word *hedonism* is derived]. You adulteresses [their selfish motives have not only hurt their interpersonal relationships with each other but have so affected their relationship with God that He views them as unfaithful spouses], do you not know that friendship with the world [the love of the world to the point of idolatry] is hostility toward God? [They have loved the world to such a degree that the love of God is not in them (see 1 John 2:15), again demonstrating that

their own desires are affecting their relationship not only with each other but also with God.] Therefore whoever wishes to be a friend of the world makes himself an enemy of God. (vv. 2–4)

On the other hand, God desires for us to desire Him with the same kind of desire with which He desires us. "Or do you think that the Scripture speaks to no purpose: 'He jealously desires the Spirit which He has made to dwell in us?'" (v. 5). The Spirit of God earnestly desires that we not displace our love for Him with a love for anything the world has to offer.

The best evidence that a Christian desires (loves) something more than he desires God is his willingness to sin against God either *in order to acquire that desire* or *because he cannot acquire it*. In John 14:15, Jesus said: "If ye love Me, keep My commandments" (KJV). One of the most common sins that demonstrate the presence of inordinate desire is anger. By identifying biblically the kind of sin that is associated with your anger, you can correct your anger not simply *externally* (e.g., temper tantrums, sarcasm, vengeance, and so on), but also *internally* (idolatry: love of pleasure, love of money, love of praise, and so on) in your heart where the anger resides.

Both James and John identified loving the world as an evidence of idolatry (James 4:4; 1 John 2:15). For identifying specific kinds of idolatry, you may find it helpful to consider those things that the Scriptures indicate that a person may love or desire or delight in too much.

For example, let's consider four of the most common idols: love of money, love of pleasure, love of approval, and love of power.

Love of Money

> But those who want to get rich fall into temptation and a snare and *many foolish and harmful desires* which plunge men into ruin and destruction. For *the love of money* is a root of all sorts of evil, and some by longing for it have wandered away from the faith, and pierced themselves with many a pang. (1 Tim. 6:9–10)

It's not the use of money or even the enjoyment of money that is a sin. It's the love of money that is *a* root (not *the* root as the KJV translators inaccurately translated it). It's one of several *root desires* identified by the Bible for which men long (covet or desire excessively) to their own harm.

Love of Pleasure

> He who *loves pleasure* will become a poor man. He who loves wine and oil will not become rich. (Prov 21:17)

> But realize this, that in the last days difficult times will come. For men will be lovers of self, lovers of money . . . *lovers of pleasure* rather than lovers of God. (2 Tim. 3:1–2, 4)

The ability to enjoy pleasure is a blessing from God, who "richly supplies us with all things to enjoy" (1 Tim. 6:17). The setting of one's heart on pleasure to the point of hedonism (taken from the same Greek word for pleasure), so that one becomes "enslaved to various lusts and pleasures" (Titus 3:3), is a heart problem of which sinful anger is often a symptom.

Love of Approval

> For they loved the *approval of men* rather than the approval of God. (John 12:43)

> But [the scribes and the Pharisees] do all their *deeds to be noticed by men*; for they broaden their phylacteries, and lengthen the tassels of their garments. And *they love the place of honor* at banquets, and the chief seats in the synagogues, and respectful greetings in the market places, and *being called by men, Rabbi*. (Matt. 23:5–7)

For us to desire the approval of others is not necessarily wrong. If it were, then to praise or commend others would be to tempt them to sin. But, as with money and pleasure (and anything else that is not inherently evil), to desire approval so much that it turns into the *love* of approval is wrong. The scribes and the Pharisees (like so many are today and down through the ages) were "approval junkies." That is, their desire for approval was so inordinate that they were in bondage to it.

"For by what a man is overcome, by this he is enslaved" (2 Peter 2:19). They wanted approval so much that they spent much of their time and effort doing those things that would bring glory from men. Even those things that were religious in nature (like prayer, fasting, and giving) were done by some with a motive to gain man's approval, for which Jesus said, "They have their reward in full" (Matt. 6:2).

The sooner you learn to desire the approval of God, the sooner the temptation to be a people-pleaser and the problem of peer pressure will be eliminated.

Love of Power (Control)

> I wrote something to the church; but Diotrephes, *who loves to be first among them*, does not accept what we say. For this reason, if I come, I will call attention to his deeds which he does, unjustly accusing us with wicked words; and not satisfied with this, *neither does he himself receive the brethren, and he forbids those who desire to do so, and puts them out of the church.* (3 John 9–10)

Diotrephes loved to hold the highest rank among the leaders in church. His love for preeminence turned him into a tyrannical leader who was even threatened by a visit from others who might disagree with him. Once again, to have a desire to manage those things over which the Lord has given you responsibility is not a sin. When, however, that desire to manage is turned into "lording it over those allotted to your charge" (1 Peter 5:3), that proper desire has turned into an idolatrous love of power.

When you continually refuse to submit to parental authority, regularly attempt to manipulate your parents, or bully your siblings and friends, you just might be doing so out of a motive that is set on controlling those things over which God has not given you authority.

Consider the thoughts recorded earlier in the Heart Journal.

That's not fair.
My mother never lets me do what I want to do.
She doesn't want me to have any fun.

She is afraid that I'll get into trouble.
She's an obsessive, overbearing terrorist.
I can't wait to get out of here.

Can you identify some possible wrong motives (idolatrous desires) out of which these thoughts might flow?

That's not fair.
My mother never lets me do what I want to do.
I can't wait to get out of here.
} LOVE OF CONTROL (the desire to usurp authority)

My mother never lets me do what I want to do.
She doesn't want me to have any fun.
} LOVE OF PLEASURE

She's an obsessive, overbearing terrorist.
} DESIRE FOR REVENGE

As you familiarize yourself with those things that the Bible specifically identifies as idolatrous, as well as with those things that you desire to the point of getting angry, you will become more proficient at using God's Word as the discerner of the thoughts and intents of your heart.

Step Four: Develop alternative biblical thoughts and motives to replace the unbiblical ones.

QUESTIONS:

What should I have said to myself when I became angry?

and What should I have wanted more than my own selfish/idolatrous desires?

It's not enough to identify and remove (put off) wrong thoughts and motives from your heart. In order for change to be biblical (effective, enduring, and pleasing to God), the Christian must *replace* sinful thoughts and motives with righteous ones. This means you must make it your goal to

137

- be pure in heart (Matt. 5:8)
- speak the truth in your heart (Ps. 15:2)
- desire truth in all of your innermost being (Ps. 51:6)
- let your mind think on whatever is true, honorable, just, pure, of good repute, excellent, and worthy of praise (Phil. 4:8)
- renew your mind (Rom. 12:2)
- be renewed in the spirit of your mind (Eph. 4:23)
- have your loins girded with truth

This is by far the most important step of the Journal because it's where repentance (change of mind) is brought to fruition. It's where correction and disciplined training in righteousness (see 2 Tim. 3:16) most concretely takes place. It's the part of this exercise that best prepares you for dealing with future provocations and temptations biblically. By identifying and rehearsing biblical alternatives to the sinful thoughts and motives of a heart that has to some extent been trained in angry practices (see 2 Peter 2:14), you can retrain yourself to want (covet) those things that are pleasing to God.

In response to the question, "What should I have said to myself when I became angry?", record as many biblically accurate alternative thoughts as you can in a reasonable amount of time (five to ten minutes at first). These alternatives should reflect three things: (1) theological accuracy (especially focusing on God's sovereignty as it relates to His ability to have prevented the provocation from occurring), (2) biblical hope (especially as it relates to His working all things together for your good, having predestined you to be conformed to the image of Christ), and (3) the putting on of those antithetical concepts to anger that are identified in Scripture (gentleness, contentment, kindness, tenderheartedness, forgiveness, and so on).

As an alternative to thinking "That's not fair!", you might consider such possible alternatives as

"The Lord could have prevented this apparent injustice, but He has a purpose in it. How can I respond to this trial in such a way that it will build character? I wonder what else He could be up to?"

or   "There really is not enough evidence to convict my mother of being unfair. I'd better not answer a matter before I hear it (Prov. 18:13)."

or   "Did I do anything to cause my mother to respond this way?"

or   "Fair or not, I've got to respond to my mother with gentleness and respect. I'd better ask the Lord for wisdom."

or   "Life is not always fair, but God is always just. I need to commit my case to Him who judges rightly."

To replace the thought, "My mother never lets me do what I want," how about some of the following options?

"What the Lord wants is more important than what I want."

or   "Perhaps He wants me to do something else right now."

or   "If I cannot respectfully persuade her to change her mind by making a biblical appeal, I will have to conclude that this is not what the Lord wants. Now, how shall I make that appeal?"

or   " 'Never' is not quite true; it seems that she does tend not to give me what I want as much as I would like, but I'd better collect more information before I even think of talking to her about that."

or   "If I want to do what I want to do so much that I sin because my mother (not to mention God Himself) will not allow me to do it, then what I want to do, I want too much."

Rather than "She doesn't want me to have any fun," perhaps these thoughts would do.

"Since she hasn't told me what her motives are in this case and since I cannot read her mind, I'd better assume the best."

or   "God is probably more concerned with my using this irritation (little trial) as an opportunity to grow as a Christian than He is with my having fun."

or   "God has given me more to do in life than just to have fun."

or "Having fun is important only as it relates to living my entire life to the glory of God; it's a means to an end, not an end in itself."

or "Sometimes, I want to have fun too much."

Instead of "She's an obsessive, overbearing terrorist," how about these thoughts?

"She's my mother, and God expects me to honor her."

or "I cannot honor her by calling her unbiblical names."

or "I'm the one who is sinning because I can't get my own way."

or "What I should do is thank her for what she has done and is doing for me and praise her for her good qualities, just as the children of the Proverbs 31 woman rise up and call her blessed."

Rather than "I can't wait to get out of here," perhaps you could respond with,

"I need endurance so that after I have done the will of God I may inherit the promise."

or "I can do all things through Christ who strengthens me."

or "My parents are divinely appointed agents through which God has determined to conform me into the image of Christ."

or "If I do not learn what the Lord wants me to learn when I'm in this circumstance, He will likely raise up similar or worse circumstances when I do get out of here to teach me what I have not learned."

or "My stay in this home is only temporary. God says I must leave someday. I will be patient while I'm here and thankful for the opportunity to grow while I'm here. I will focus my attention on how I can minister to my parents and please them as long as I'm under their authority."

The last question in the Heart Journal is the question, "What should I have wanted more than my own selfish desires?"

The ultimate answer to this question in every case ought to be to glorify God. This concept may be expressed in a variety of ways. Before we identify some of the forms of motivation that most glorify God, let's consider some of those delights, loves, and longings that Scripture encourages us to develop as believers in Jesus Christ. (Incidentally, it could be argued that if a person lacks these desires, he might not be a Christian at all. Such a person would do well to examine himself to see whether he is in the faith; see 2 Cor. 13:5).

A Christian's first love should be a love for the Lord his God that exudes from his heart, mind, soul, and strength (Luke 10:27). This ought to be the supreme motive for everything that a Christian does. He may additionally have good and noble motives in his heart, but this love must be preeminent.

A Christian's motive should be to love his neighbor as (with the same intensity with which) he loves himself. As every man naturally "nourishes and cherishes" himself (Eph. 5:29), so the Christian is to love his neighbor to the same degree (Luke 10:27).

In addition to these two "righteous loves," we may categorize the other appropriate loves spoken of by name in the Bible. These, of course, are proper to the degree that they are subordinate to loving God. Here is a partial list.

1. The Love of the Word of God (Ps. 119:140)
2. The Love of Wisdom (Prov. 4:6; 8:17)
3. The Love of Mercy (Mic. 6:8)
4. The Love of Truth (Zech. 8:19; 2 Thess. 2:10)
5. The Love of Peace (Zech. 8:19)
6. The Love of That which is Good (Amos 5:15)
7. The Love of the Lord's Return (2 Tim. 4:8)
8. The Love of Life (not one's own) (1 Peter 3:10)
9. The Love of Light (John 3:19)
10. The Love of One's Spouse (Eph. 5:25)

By training yourself to answer this final question in the *Heart Journal*, you will be developing proper motivation and will be training yourself to set your affections on the things above rather than on the things that are on earth (Col. 3:2).

In answering this last question, you will discover a number of the appropriate alternative desires in which you ought to delight, love, pursue, set your affection, covet, and so forth. You will be using the "momentary, light affliction" to "produce an eternal weight of glory far beyond all comparison" as with the eyes of your heart you learn to "look not at the temporal things which are seen, but at the eternal things which are not seen" (see 2 Cor. 4:17–18).

In every situation that once brought sinful anger to your heart as a result of delighting too much in some temporal pleasure, you can train yourself to delight increasingly in doing God's revealed will. "I delight to do Thy will, O my God; Thy law is within my heart" (Ps. 40:8).

Rather than asking yourself, "What do I want to do?", you can begin to start asking, "What does the Lord want me to do?"

What then are some alternative biblical motives (desires) with which you can replace the idolatrous ones you discover in your heart? How can the desires to love, glorify, and obey God be expressed so that they may prayerfully be cultivated to maturity? What are the proper answers to the question, "What should I have wanted more than my own selfish desires?" Below I have listed a few to get you started (next to each response I've suggested a portion of Scripture you may memorize to assist you in cultivating each God-honoring motive).

Righteous Desires *I could have wanted:*	Related Scripture
To love and glorify God by . . .	Matthew 5:16
To delight in doing God's will which was . . .	Psalm 40:8
To be more like Jesus Christ in this way . . .	2 Corinthians 3:18
To love my neighbor as myself . . .	Matthew 22:34–40
To acquire wisdom and understanding . . .	Proverbs 4:5–9
To honor and obey my parents . . .	Ephesians 6:1–3
To delight in God's Word . . .	Psalm 1:2
To delight more in what I can give to others than in what I can get . . .	Acts 20:35
To minister to others . . .	Matthew 20:25–28
To offer a blessing . . .	1 Peter 3:8–16
To demonstrate to my parents that I'm trustworthy . . .	Proverbs 20:6

Do you remember our example of a teenager who was complaining to his parents about not being allowed to visit a friend due to prior commitments? Let's take another look at the thoughts we've been analyzing, this time trying to identify the potential wrong desires that may have generated them, along with their corresponding biblically adjusted thoughts.

That's not fair.
My mother never lets me do what I want to do.
I can't wait to get out of here.

} LOVE OF CONTROL
(the desire to usurp authority)

New thoughts and motives:	I desire:
"Life is not always fair, but God is always just."	To delight in doing God's will.
"I need to commit myself to Him who judges righteously."	To be more like Jesus Christ.
"What the Lord wants is more important than what I want. Perhaps He wants me to do something else right now."	To honor and obey my parents.
"My parents are divinely appointed instruments through which God has sovereignly determined to conform me to the image of Christ."	To control only those things for which I'm biblically responsible to control, and to trust God to work all things (especially those things I cannot control) for good.

My mother never lets me do what I want to do. } LOVE OF PLEASURE
She doesn't want me to have any fun.

New thoughts and motives:	I desire:
"What the Lord wants is more important than what I want. If I want to do what I want so much that I sin because my mother (not to mention God Himself) will not let me do it, then what I want to do, I want to do too much."	To know Christ, the power of His resurrection, the fellowship of His suffering.
"Having fun is important only as it relates to living my entire life to the glory of God." (It's all a means to an end, not an end in and of itself.)	To be holy more than to be happy.
God is probably more concerned with using this trial as an avenue to help me grow as a Christian than He is with my having fun.	To please and glorify God.
	To be conformed to the image of Christ (which will bring lasting happiness and eternal pleasure.)

She's an obsessive, overbearing terrorist. } DESIRE FOR REVENGE

New thoughts and motives:	I desire:
"She's my mother and God expects me to honor her. I cannot honor her by calling her unbiblical names. What I should be doing is blessing her, thanking her for what she has done and is doing for me, and praising her for her good qualities."	To honor my parents.
	To glorify God.
	To bless others.
	To do good and to be good.

Here are a few examples of completed Heart Journals, which parallel the scenarios used to complete the Anger Journals in chapter 7. Remember that these are only examples and are not uniquely correct. Any variety of possible answers exist that are just as, if not more, correct.

Because it can take a considerable amount of time to completely fill out this journal, let me again suggest that you not consider doing the bulk of the work during your regular time of Bible study. To do this, answer questions one and two as soon after each anger-generating episode as you reasonably can. Then the next morning (or whenever your next "quiet time" is), open your Bible and concordance (and any other Bible study tool you think would be helpful), and get to work answering questions three and four. Remember, the more Scripture you study and internalize in the process, the more the Holy Spirit will have to work with as He transforms you by the renewing of your mind.

HEART JOURNAL

1. What happened that provoked me to anger? (What were the circumstances that led to my becoming angry?)

When I asked Mom if she would buy a paint gun for me that was on sale at Walmart, she said, "No." She said that the last time she bought me one, I used it to shoot at my little brother and the family pets when I got mad at them.

2. What did I say to myself (in my heart) when I became angry? (What did I want, desire, or long for when I became angry?)

I'm the best shot in town. I've got to have that gun so I can show my friends how good I am. She'll never trust me with anything ever again. I'll make her pay by leaving her to carry the packages to the car by herself. (I wanted the paint gun so that I could have fun and show off to my friends.)

3. What does the Bible say about what I said to myself when I became angry? (What does the Bible say about what I wanted when I became angry?)

The Bible says my thoughts were proud, vindictive, rash, boastful, unloving, and presumptuous. (The Bible says that my desires were idolatrous in that I was a "lover of pleasure" more than a "lover of God," and I "loved the approval of man" more than the approval of God.)

4. What should I have said to myself when I became angry? (What should I have wanted more than my own selfish/idolatrous desires?)

I guess He doesn't want me to have this paint gun right now. Perhaps the Lord knows that if I had it now, I would be tempted to use it to gain approval rather than to glorify Him. When I can demonstrate over time that I can control my anger, my mother will likely let me have it. Rather than throwing my usual temper tantrum, I'm going to bless Mom by helping her carry the packages to the car.

HEART JOURNAL

1. What happened that provoked me to anger? (What were the circumstances that led to my becoming angry?)

   I was shooting baskets in our driveway when my dad stuck his head out the back door and insisted that I come in to begin doing my homework. He told my friend who was shooting with me to come back tomorrow.

2. What did I say to myself (in my heart) when I became angry? (What did I want, desire, or long for when I became angry?)

   • I'm right in the middle of a game.
   • I can't believe he's spoiling my fun.
   • I hate it when he does that.
   • He's always running my friends off.
   • It's my life! Why doesn't he let me do what I want to do?

   (I wanted to finish playing basketball with my friends. I wanted to have fun. I wanted to decide when I should play and when I should do my homework.)

3. What does the Bible say about what I said to myself when I became angry? (What does the Bible say about what I wanted when I became angry?)

   The Bible says my thoughts were sinful:

   • Selfish
   • Hateful
   • Dishonest
   • Rebellious

   The Bible says my desires were idolatrous in that I was a "lover of pleasure" more than a "lover of God." Also, since I desired to "control" that which He did not give me the responsibility to control, I "loved to be in control" more than I loved God.

4. What should I have said to myself when I became angry? (What should I have wanted more than my own selfish/idolatrous desires?)

I could have said to myself, "I'm right in the middle of a game. Perhaps I can appeal to Dad to let me finish the game before I start my homework. If not, I'll have to assume that the Lord has other plans for my time. One thing is sure: my having fun is not as important to God as honoring my father is. It will be nice when my father trusts me to keep my own schedule and to make my own decisions. The more I obey him, the more likely he will be to trust me." (I should have desired to love God more than desiring the pleasure of playing basketball. I should have desired to be more Christlike and submitted to my father's will rather than sinfully imposing my will upon his.)

HEART JOURNAL

1. What happened that provoked me to anger? (What were the circumstances that led to my becoming angry?)

   I was invited to a sleepover with four of my friends. When I asked if I could go, my parents said "no." I tried to appeal (before I heard their reasons for saying no) but they wouldn't let me.

2. What did I say to myself (in my heart) when I became angry? (What did I want, desire, or long for when I became angry?)

   He always says "no." I wonder if he even remembers what the word "yes" sounds like. He never lets me have fun with my friends unless he has checked everything out at least 16 times! He is not happy unless he micromanages every little detail of my life. Now I'm going to have to listen to all my friends boast about how much fun they had and tease me for not being able to go to yet another fun-filled event. (I wanted to have fun with my friends. I didn't want to have to listen to all my friends tell me later how much fun they had without me at the party.)

3. What does the Bible say about what I said to myself when I became angry? (What does the Bible say about what I wanted when I became angry?)

   The Bible says my thoughts were dishonest, resentful, slanderous (falsely accusative), and bitterly sarcastic. The Bible convicts me of being idolatrous both as a "lover of pleasure" more than a "lover of God" and as a "man-pleaser" more than a "God-pleaser." And my motives were proud—not to mention selfish—for overreacting to the thought of being teased and for not wanting to rejoice with my friends. I know that I probably would have had a lot of fun. I guess that means I was also being envious of them.

4. What should I have said to myself when I became angry? (What should I have wanted more than my own selfish/idolatrous desires?)

Apparently the Lord doesn't want me to go to this party for some reason. Perhaps He is protecting me from something or there is something better for me at home. Maybe if I show my dad that I can take a "no" answer with a good attitude this time, he will be more willing to let me do something fun the next time. I should have wanted to please the Lord more than to please myself. I should have been more willing to do His will than to do my own. I should have wanted to "rejoice with those who rejoice." (I should have focused more on, and been thankful for, how much fun my friends were going to have rather than on the fun I was going to miss. I could have looked forward to being able to spend more time with my Dad.)

HEART JOURNAL

1. What happened that provoked me to anger? (What were the circumstances that led to my becoming angry?)

    The youth group at our church was going to see a movie on Saturday evening. The movie was to end later than my normal curfew. When I asked if I could go, my parents said they'd talk about it. The answer was "no" because Dad wanted to make sure my heart (and my body) were ready for church on Sunday morning.

2. What did I say to myself (in my heart) when I became angry? (What did I want, desire, or long for when I became angry?)

    - I can't believe he's spoiling my fun.
    - What's the big deal about getting my heart ready for church?
    - I'm sure it will be real easy to get my heart ready now that he has made me resentful.
    - Besides, I'm sure I will be ready to worship the Lord in the morning while I'm grieving over all the fun I missed out on at the movie!

    (I wanted to have fun with my friends. I wanted to be treated like a responsible adult who is mature enough to make her own decisions.)

3. What does the Bible say about what I said to myself when I became angry? (What does the Bible say about what I wanted when I became angry?)

    The Bible says my thoughts were sinful: selfish, bitter, hateful, and irreverent. (The Bible says my desires were idolatrous in that I was behaving more like a "lover of pleasure" than a "lover of God." Also, I wanted my parents to give me the privilege of being treated like an adult without having to earn it. So I guess that means I was also being impatient and maybe a bit lazy.)

152

4. What should I have said to myself when I became angry? (What should I have wanted more than my own selfish/idolatrous desires?)

I could have said to myself, "Dad is probably right. I've got six other days to have fun. I should be thankful for a father who loves God as much as he does (and who loves me enough to do what is best for me.) I'm glad my friends will be able to go. I will pray that they will both have fun and be alert for church in the morning, and that my disappointment will not turn into bitterness." (I should have desired to obey my father more than to have fun with my friends. I should have been willing to wait for my parents to decide when I'm mature enough to make these kinds of decisions for myself—or at least have been willing to prove to them that I am that mature.)

10

UNDOING DISRESPECT

I MENTIONED PREVIOUSLY that as a rule, nothing provokes parents to anger more quickly than disrespect. There is something about an insolent son or daughter that upsets a parent and incites him to action—and often the wrong kind of action. In this chapter we will explore what disrespect is, how it's displayed, why you might be motivated to show it, and what you can do to correct it.

Disrespect is first and foremost an attitude of the heart. It is rooted in the sins of pride and selfishness. It's a root out of which flows all manner of other sins (e.g., resentment, abusive speech, and hatred). Disrespect has to do with not esteeming others more highly than yourself. It's the belief that you are wiser, smarter, cooler, or otherwise better than others. Beyond this, it's not giving others the honor that they are due and, in some cases, it's showing contempt for them. Because disrespect is rooted in pride, the conceited person loathes humbling him or herself in the presence of others by treating them as if they were in any way superior. Yet, ironically enough, the disrespectful person selfishly longs for others to esteem him or her highly.

"OK, I admit it. I'm proud and selfish. But I still don't think *everybody* deserves my respect."

Perhaps not, but people in positions of authority do—especially parents.

HONOR YOUR FATHER AND MOTHER (which is the first commandment with a promise), SO THAT IT MAY BE WELL WITH YOU, AND THAT YOU MAY LIVE LONG ON THE EARTH. (Eph. 6:2–3)

Paul here is citing the fifth commandment. He is reminding you that you have been commanded by God to honor your parents. The word *honor* means to revere, to hold in awe, to place a high value on, to venerate. As you can see, this again is a heart attitude. It's out of this internal attitude that obedience naturally and freely flows, along with all manner of gracious forms of communication. As we saw earlier, "you can't fake it if it's not in there." So before I help you to identify and correct any external disrespectful attitudes that you demonstrate to your folks, I must ask you to confess and forsake the disrespectful attitude that you may have toward your parents in your heart.

This fifth commandment is the first one with a two-part promise attached to it. The first part is that the quality of your life will be enhanced: "that it may be well with you." The second part is that the quantity of your life will be extended: "and that you may live long on the earth."

"That all sounds good, but you obviously don't know my parents. How can God expect me to honor them when they consistently do things that cause me to lose respect for them? They really are hypocrites. They don't practice what they preach."

Did you know that the apostle Paul faced the same dilemma? One day he was escorted into a room of religious authorities (the Sanhedrin) who were about to falsely accuse him of wrongdoing. As he stood in their midst between two guards, he began speaking. "Brethren, I have lived my life with a perfectly good conscience before God up to this day" (Acts 23:1). Then someone in the council stood up and ordered the guards standing beside him to slug him in the mouth. Pretty hypocritical, wouldn't you say? Paul thought so, too. "Then Paul said to him, 'God is going to strike you, you whitewashed wall! And do you sit to try me according to the Law, and in violation of the Law order me to be struck?' " (v. 3).

At this point Paul had this guy pegged as a first-class hypocrite—a "whitewashed wall." He made an accurate assessment of his personality. Then something quite remarkable happened. Others in the room began to confront Paul as they pointed out to him that the man he had just publicly ridiculed and called a whitewashed wall had a divinely appointed *position* that went along with his despicable *personality*. "But the bystanders said, 'Do you revile God's high priest?' "(v. 4).

As soon as Paul realized that the man he had just (accurately) reviled and assessed as a hypocrite was the high priest, he showed contrition. "And Paul said, 'I was not aware, brethren, that he was high priest; for it is written, "YOU SHALL NOT SPEAK EVIL OF A RULER OF YOUR PEOPLE" ' " (v. 5).

You may be right in your assessment of your parents' personality. They may be very hard to respect. But you cannot lose sight of the fact that God has given them a position of authority that you must honor. You must learn to salute the uniform that God has given your folks even if you believe it's *six sizes too big* for them. There are ways for you to address the fact that they don't fill it out very well. We will cover these in chapter 13.

But we are getting a bit ahead of ourselves. Let's get to the question of why you are disrespectful.

WHY AM I DISRESPECTFUL?

There is a variety of reasons why teenagers struggle with disrespect. Most of them stem from the sins of pride and selfishness.

"Do nothing from *selfishness* or *empty conceit*, but with humility of mind let each of you regard one another as more important than himself" (Phil. 2:3). Notice that you are to esteem others (not just your parents) higher than yourself. As for your own motives, could it be that in your heart you don't want them telling you what to do, so you give yourself a reason to justify your selfish desire for premature independence by reminding yourself of how unworthy your parents are of your respect?

That may or may not be what motivates you, so here are some additional reasons teens find to show disrespect to their folks. Put a check in the box next to each one that applies to you.

Motivations behind my disrespectful attitude toward my parents are often:

☐ To divert their attention (to keep from having to do what my parents ask of me)

☐ To get even (to vindictively pay them back for not giving me what I want)

☐ To protest (to teach them that "they can't treat me that way")

☐ To be myself (to help them to see that "this is just the way I am, and I'm not going to change the way I talk for anyone")

☐ To manipulate them (to evoke a sinful response from them so that they will feel guilty and give me what I want)

☐ To register a complaint (to express my disapproval for what they have done or said)

☐ To test the limits (to see how far I can push my parents before they tell me to stop)

☐ To see who's in control (to discover the extent to which I can manage my parents)

☐ To justify my contempt (to establish the fact that I have good reason not to respect them)

☐ Other: _____

☐ No real ulterior motive (it's just the way I have learned to communicate with them)

"I think I know what comes next. You are going to ask me, with God's help, to somehow replace these wrong desires with their 'biblical alternatives.' "

Exactly. So what do you think those desires might be?

"I have no idea, but I'm sure you are going to tell me."

It would be my pleasure. (By the way, did I detect a note of sarcasm in that statement?) As with everything you do, your ultimate motive should be to glorify God: "Whatever you do, do all to the glory of God" (1 Cor. 10:31). So then, here are some other good things that might motivate you to honor your parents.

☐ The promise of a better quality of life (see Eph. 6:3)
☐ The promise of a lengthier life (see Eph. 6:3)

☐ To repay your parents for all they have done for you

☐ To build more humility into your life (and so to access God's grace)

☐ To build more love (the antidote to selfishness) into your life

☐ To be an example of Christ to others (especially to your siblings)

☐ To prepare for marriage (husbands and wives are both commanded to show respect to their spouses; see 1 Peter 3:2–7)

☐ To be a more gracious person in general (see Eph. 4:29; Col. 4:6)

☐ To obtain more rewards in heaven (see 1 Tim. 4:8)

Make these items a matter of prayer. Ask God to give you a heart filled with respect for your parents and for all authorities. Make a commitment to change the way you think about and respond to your parents. By so adjusting your thoughts and actions, and with the right motivation, you should find that your feelings for your parents change rather quickly.

HOW AM I DISRESPECTFUL TO MY PARENTS?

Now that we have examined your motives, let's look a little closer at your words, attitudes, and actions. How exactly have you been disrespectful to your folks? (What have been your favorite means of showing disrespect to them?) Put a check in the box next to the disrespectful behaviors below that you are most prone to utilize.

☐ By refusing to talk to them
☐ By rolling my eyes at them
☐ By raising my voice at them
☐ By calling them names
☐ By telling them "no"
☐ By threatening them
☐ By looking at them angrily
☐ By withholding affection
☐ By scoffing
☐ By willfully disobeying them
☐ By cursing them

☐ By being rude and unmannerly
☐ By refusing to be corrected
☐ By interrupting them when they are speaking
☐ By not being attentive to them when they are speaking to me
☐ By walking away when they are speaking to me
☐ By murmuring and complaining against them
☐ By comparing them unfavorably to the parents of my friends
☐ By having a condescending attitude
☐ By contradicting them in front of others
☐ By making them out to be ridiculous or contemptible

Show this list to your parents, asking their forgiveness for the things you have checked off. Then ask them if there are any other disrespectful things you have done for which you need to ask forgiveness. Finally, ask them to call to your attention any times that you use these disrespectful forms of communication in the future.

With what will you replace these discourteous deeds? Here are a few suggestions. Rate them in order of ease (and comfort) to difficulty (and discomfort), using this rating scale.

5—Easy 4—Comfortable 3—Not Easy 2—Uncomfortable 1—Difficult

_____ By being attentive to them
_____ By being affectionate to them
_____ By expressing gratitude
_____ By commending them to my friends
_____ By obeying their instructions
_____ By responding, "Yes, sir" or "No, ma'am"
_____ By smiling at them
_____ By asking for their opinion
_____ By using terms of endearment
_____ By following their instructions
_____ By using good manners
_____ By seeking to spend time with them

_____ By praying for them
_____ By honoring them publicly
_____ By quickly admitting when I am wrong
_____ By buying them (or making them) an unexpected gift of appreciation
_____ By offering to help them with their chores
_____ By telephoning them if I'm going to be home later than expected
_____ By speaking to them in a warm and pleasant tone of voice
_____ By carefully choosing gracious words
_____ By holding my tongue when I'm too angry to speak graciously
_____ By cheerfully accepting a "no" answer to one of my requests
_____ By looking directly at them when they are speaking to me

HOW TO SHOW RESPECT TO PARENTS

Here are some final thoughts on what you can do to better develop a more respectful attitude toward your parents.

1. Remember that you will not always have to _obey_ your parents, but you _will_ always have to honor them.
2. Learn to distinguish between their personality and their position. You will always have people in positions of authority over you. (Learn this lesson early, and it will help to spare you from a lot of misery later in life.)
3. Learn to esteem your parents more highly than you do yourself. Paul told the Romans to "outdo one another in showing honor" (Rom. 12:10 ESV). Do not be wise in your own eyes. Do not presume that God has given you more wisdom in a few years than He has given to your parents in a much longer period of time.
4. Learn to listen actively and to not interrupt. Much disrespect can be avoided by simply waiting until your parents have finished making their point before you say anything.
5. Tell your parents right up front that you will do what they ask. If you want to disarm them from hastily cutting off your requests

due to a bad attitude, try letting them know *immediately* that you intend to obey them. This will help to assure them that the passionate discussion that may follow will not be accompanied by a defiant attitude on your part.

6. If you are angry, tell your folks *politely* and ask them to help you. "Dad, I have decided that I'm going to do what you say no matter how much I disagree. Will you please help me to express my concerns without getting angry by listening carefully to my perspective?" Or perhaps something like this: "Mom, I want to have a good attitude about this, but I'm not succeeding right now because I think you are not understanding my point of view. Will you please pray for me that I will be able to talk to you about this without getting sinfully angry?"

7. If you blow it, stop and ask for forgiveness *immediately*. You may be amazed how quickly asking for forgiveness for your own disrespectful attitude can turn around a conversation that is going south.

8. Learn how to use the appeal process. Chapter 12 will provide you with an additional resource that may help you to approach your parents once they have made a decision.

9. Work hard at being patient and at forbearing with your parents as they correct you. It's their God-given responsibility (see Prov. 19:18; 23:13–14; Eph. 6:4). It's also a demonstration of their love for you (see Prov. 13:24; Heb. 12:4–11).

10. Express gratitude for the fact that your parents love you enough to do what they believe is best for you. You don't have to agree with their reasoning to believe that they love you and are trying to give you what you need.

11. Choose friends who are characterized by being respectful. Avoid close friendships with those who are characterized by contempt for authority. "He who walks with wise men will be wise, but the companion of fools will suffer harm" (Prov. 13:20).

12. Learn to delight in their company. Do you enjoy spending time conversing with your friends? Sure you do. Well, how about

investing some of your spare time talking to your folks, "picking their brains" about something that they enjoy (even if it's not on your top ten list of exciting things to talk about). It just might not be as boring as you think.

13. Imitate your parents in all that is good.[1] Look for and emulate all those Christlike characteristics that you see in your parents. As you read in your Bible, notice those character traits that your parents possess (e.g., the virtuous woman in Proverbs 31; the fruit of the Spirit in Galatians 5:22–23). Commend them for being such a good example in those areas. Ask them to help you be more like them.

14. Remember that you too are a sinner. Your folks are not the only ones in your family who are in need of God's forgiveness and grace. They have forgiven you of plenty. You are obligated to forgive them. Is it right to be angry with them for doing what the Bible says they should do (helping you to learn how to deal properly with your sin problems) rather than honoring them for doing what God requires?

15. Keep in mind that by honoring your parents, you will be blessed according to Scripture; by dishonoring them, you will be cursed (see Gen. 9:22, 25; Prov. 30:17). To physically or verbally abuse a parent was a capital offense under the Old Testament economy (Ex. 21:15, 17; Lev. 20:7). Check it out.

---

1. Richard Baxter, "A Christian Directory," in *The Practical Works of Richard Baxter*, vol. 1 (repr., Ligonier, PA: Soli Deo Gloria, 1990), 456.

11

MANAGING MANIPULATION

HERE IS A LITTLE TEST for you to take to see how good you are at manipulating your folks.

RATING SCALE

Never or hardly ever	5
Seldom	4
Occasionally	3
Frequently	2
Almost always	1
Always	0

MANIPULATION TEST

1. My parents have to repeat and/or reword instructions before I'm willing to follow them. _____

2. When my parents ask me to do something, I ask, "Why?" _____

3. I pressure my parents to justify their decisions to me. _____

4. My parents express weariness or frustration over certain "topics" that I want to discuss over and over again with them. _____

5. I play one parent against the other. I know that if one of them says "no," I can always appeal to the other. _____

6. I selfishly try to make my parents feel guilty when they don't give me what I want. _____

7. I lie to my parents. _____

8. I try to influence the disciplinary process so that I can be disciplined almost entirely by one parent (who is more lenient than the other). _____

9. My parents rescind disciplinary actions (or lift restrictions) because of my incessant appeals. _____

10. I pressure my parents to negotiate and/or compromise their values with me. _____

11. I cleverly sidetrack my parents with distractions when they attempt to discipline me. _____

12. I try to obligate my parents to behave a certain way by telling them what they should, ought to, or must do (other than for biblical reasons). _____

13. When I want something from my parents, I try to motivate them to give it to me without telling them directly what I want. _____

14. I'm able to procrastinate by cleverly using numerous stall tactics when my parents assign me a responsibility. _____

15. I'm able to play on my parents' emotions in order to get what I want. _____

16. I try to intimidate my parents. _____

17. I successfully thwart my parents' attempts at instruction and discipline by my unwillingness to cooperate. _____

18. I'm so tenacious in wanting my own way that my parents either give in to my desires or give up on trying to resist me. _____

19. I continue to beg and plead to have my way after I've been denied an appeal. _____

20. I'm more disobedient and disrespectful in front
of others when I know such behavior is likely to
embarrass my parents.   _____

SCORING YOUR TEST

Add up the total number of points to determine your score. Based
on one hundred percent, if your total score is ninety or better, you have
no problem with manipulating your parents. (You have a problem with
dishonesty, but not with manipulation.) If your total score is between
75 and 90, you are in some measure manipulating your folks. If your
total score is below 75, you are very likely manipulating them to a great
extent. The lower your score, the greater your effort should be to learn
and apply the principles in this chapter.

WHAT IS MANIPULATION?

Webster's dictionary defines *manipulate* as "to control or play upon
by artful, unfair, or insidious means."[1] For a Christian, manipulation is
using means of controlling or influencing another that are unbiblical.
More specifically, manipulation is often an attempt to gain control of
another individual or situation by inciting an emotional reaction rather
than a biblical response from that individual. In the tenth chapter of Luke,
for example, Martha "was distracted with all her preparations; and she
came up to Him [Jesus], and said, 'Lord, do You not care that my sister
has left me to do all the serving alone? Then tell her to help me' " (v. 40).

Martha wanted assistance with her food preparations and was
frustrated (angry) that her sister had left her to do all the serving by
herself. Rather than telling the Lord exactly what she wanted (help with
the cooking), she first attempted to play on His emotions (sympathy and
perhaps guilt). "Do you not care?" Another element of manipulation
can be seen in Martha's response. Here she was attempting to motivate
someone to fulfill her personal desires without clearly stating them.
An appeal for sympathy, rightly expressed, is not necessarily wrong
as long as the true desire behind such an appeal is also expressed (in

---

1. *Merriam-Webster's Collegiate Dictionary*, 11th ed., s.v. "manipulate."

this case, Martha's desire for help). To do otherwise is usually dishonest because it's concealing necessary information from the person to whom the appeal is made.

Before looking at how Jesus responded to this and other manipulative ploys by friends and foes alike, I would like to further develop the concept of emotional manipulation.

The following chart will serve to simplify and illustrate the ways and means of teenage manipulation. The first column, "Manipulative Behavior," lists some of the more common ways in which teens tend to manipulate their parents. You may or may not be consciously aware that you are being manipulative. I say this because from a very young age (even before you could pronounce the word *manipulation*, let alone know what it was), you may have trained yourself to get what you want by being manipulative. All you may have known is that by doing or saying certain things you could get what you wanted. So you practiced and practiced your manipulative behaviors, perhaps not even knowing until later (if at all) that you had become a manipulator.

The second column, "Desired Emotional Response," pinpoints what you may want your manipulative behavior to produce within your folks. Again, remember that you may have practiced your manipulative ways for so long that at any given moment you may not even be aware of what your desires really are.

The third column, "Parental Reaction," identifies the foolish responses of a parent who has just been successfully manipulated by his teen. In *The Heart of Anger*, I show your parents how to identify and correct these unbiblical responses. But remember, to the extent that your folks do any of these things at your provocation, God will hold you partly responsible for being a stumbling block to them (see Rom. 14:13–21; 1 Cor. 8:9–13).

The fourth column, "Desired Controlling Effect," is the result that you hope your manipulative behavior will have on your parents. You *will* most likely be aware of this one, regardless of how conscious you are of the items in the first three columns.

The fifth column, "Sinful Motives," suggests possible motives for the manipulation. That is, it specifies those potential desires that may be so intense that you are willing to resort to manipulation (sin) in order to obtain what you want. These motives are suggested not only so that you might better understand the source of your manipulation, but also to help you identify and correct the problem at its source.

ELEMENTS OF MANIPULATIVE BEHAVIOR

Manipulative Behavior	Desired Emotional Response	Parental Reaction	Desired Controlling Effect	Sinful Motives
Accusations	Guilt	Defend self	To procrastinate	Love of pleasure
Criticisms	Shame	Justify actions	To avoid obligation	Love of power
Crying	Embarrassment	Blame shifting	To change parent's mind	Love of praise
"Why" questions	Hurt	Answer "why" questions	To lower parent's standard	Love of money
Obligatory statements	Anger	Yelling Back	To rescind parental punishment	Love of _____ (whatever)
Sulking				
Pouting				
Whining				
Withholding affection				
Cold shoulder				

Christ never answered a fool with a foolish response. He never fought folly with folly. In communicating with fools, He never employed communication forms that violated Scripture. Although He did respond to foolishness, He did not respond in kind. In other words, He did not allow the fool with whom He was talking to drag Him down to his level by playing the same sinful communication games as His opponent.

What He did do when responding to foolish verbiage was to show the fool his own foolishness. Those who approached Christ with the intent to manipulate Him (often by trying to make Him look foolish), walked away realizing how foolish they themselves were.

A BIBLICAL RESPONSE TO FOOLISHNESS

Solomon spoke of the emotional agony associated with parenting a child who was so filled with folly that he would be classified scripturally as a "fool." "He who begets a fool does so to his sorrow, and the father of a fool has no joy" (Prov. 17:21). "A foolish son is a grief to his father, and bitterness to her who bore him" (Prov. 17:25). There is a response to foolishness mentioned in the book of Proverbs, out of which flows the essence of Christ's adeptness at dealing with manipulators. He consistently employed the wisdom of Proverbs in dealing with foolish requests, setups, and attempts to control Him. Proverbs 26:4–5 says, "Do not answer a fool according to his folly, lest you also be like him. Answer a fool as his folly deserves, lest he be wise in his own eyes." In the original *Heart of Anger*, I unpack for Christian parents how Christ employed this passage repeatedly with those who tried to manipulate Him. My task in this book is different. My desire is to help you learn how to use appropriate means (rather than manipulative ones) to make requests of your parents and to encourage you to respond correctly should your requests be turned down.

The following chart (originally designed to help parents) contrasts the difference between answering a manipulative child according to his folly and answering a manipulative child as his folly deserves.

ANSWERING A MANIPULATIVE CHILD

... according to his folly (Prov. 26:4)	... as his folly deserves (Prov. 26:5)
The parent is drawn into a conflict by his child.	The parent is in control of the conversation with his child.
The child is allowed to employ sinful manipulative behaviors successfully.	The child is confronted biblically when sinful manipulative behaviors are employed.
The parent reacts with a snappy comeback motivated by emotions other than love for his child.	The parent responds out of love with a well-thought-out biblical answer that aims to drive out foolishness from the heart of his child.
The parent resorts to defending himself, justifying his actions, blame-shifting, answering "why" questions, argumentation, etc.	The parent identifies and effectively puts an end to his child's manipulative behavior.
The parent allows his child to terminate the conversation by having the last word before biblical correction has taken place.	The parent does not allow the conversation to end until biblical discipline and/or correction has taken place so that the child acknowledges and repents of his sin.
The parent walks away feeling guilty, intimidated, frustrated, exasperated, like a failure, and/or out of control.	The parent walks away confident that by God's grace he is in control of and successfully accomplishing the training of his child.
The child walks away with the satisfaction of knowing that he has punished or manipulated his parent.	The child walks away knowing that his parent has successfully thwarted his attempts at disrespect and manipulation.

That's probably enough about that. Let's take a look at how you can do a better job of approaching your parents without having to resort to manipulation.

"Wait a minute, Lou! Aren't you going to tell us what Jesus did to keep people from manipulating Him?"

I told you, that information was intended for your parents, not for you.

"But that's not fair! You got me all fired up about this stuff and now you're going to leave me hanging."

Are you trying to manipulate me? Why don't you try that question again? You already know how I will respond to the "That's not fair!" remark.

"OK, I'll try it again. Lou, I know that you wrote this anti-manipulation stuff for parents, and I know that I should be more concerned about not manipulating my folks than I am about how they ought to respond to my manipulation, but I really would like to know this information because I've got friends who manipulate me. Besides, if I understand how Jesus kept people from manipulating Him, it might give me additional motivation to not put my parents in a position to do to me what He did to them."

All right. But I can give you only a *very* abbreviated treatment of the topic. I devoted two entire chapters to this in the first book.

Scripture records many examples of individuals who attempted to manipulate Christ. Not one person ever succeeded! In studying Christ's responses to those manipulative individuals, I have identified at least two anti-manipulation techniques that Jesus often used. These two techniques are frequently found together, but almost always at least one of them was employed.

Before explaining what they are, I must first give a warning. Christ could not sin. His motives, therefore, for responding to the foolish requests and questions of those who wanted to manipulate him were impeccable. He always wanted to please and glorify His Father. For you to attempt to use the biblical resources that you are about to learn for selfish ends is wrong. To do so would not only be evil (the very evil you are trying to deal with biblically: manipulation), it would not be blessed by God and would likely backfire. In other words, to use biblical weapons (which were meant for the purpose of fighting evil) in order to get what *you* want rather than what *God* wants will be viewed by Him as sin; it would be nothing more than a gimmick to manipulate others, including God Himself. If you expect God to bless you in your efforts to keep others from manipulating you, you must be certain that your motives are unselfish before you attempt to use these resources.

Now that you've been warned, I will briefly describe these two anti-manipulation devices to you. They are as follows:

1. An appeal is made to the manipulator to fulfill certain biblical responsibilities that he has neglected to fulfill.
2. An appeal is made to God's Word (or at least to God's will as found in God's Word) as the standard for judgment of the manipulator.

For instance, getting back to the story of Mary and Martha found in the tenth chapter of Luke, how did Christ deal with Martha's attempt to pressure Him into giving her what she wanted?

> Now as they were traveling along, He entered a certain village; and a woman named Martha welcomed Him into her home. And she had a sister called Mary, who moreover was listening to the Lord's word, seated at His feet. But Martha was distracted with all her preparations; and she came up to Him, and said, "Lord, do You not care that my sister has left me to do all the serving alone? Then tell her to help me." But the Lord answered and said to her, "Martha, Martha, you are worried and bothered about so many things; but only a few things are necessary, really only one, for Mary has chosen the good part, which shall not be taken away from her." (vv. 38–42)

First, He made an appeal to her personal responsibilities. He said, "Martha, Martha, you are worried and bothered about so many things; but only a few things are necessary, really only one." Jesus said elsewhere that His disciples ought not to worry (Matt. 6:25) or be troubled

(John 14:1). Therefore, Martha was not fulfilling at least two biblical responsibilities, and Jesus reproved her. He reminded her that her only necessary responsibility was to sit at His feet and hear the Word of God.

Second, He made a subtle yet definite appeal to God's will. He said, "Only a few things are necessary, really only one, for Mary has chosen the good part, which shall not be taken away from her." During Jesus' own temptation when He was in the wilderness for forty days, He said, "Man shall not live on bread alone, but on every word that proceeds out of the mouth of God" (Matt. 4:4; Luke 4:4). Consequently, Mary, who was feasting on the Word of God, was commended for doing the good (right) thing. The fact that Jesus called what Mary had chosen to do "necessary" and "good" implies that she was doing God's will.

That's all you're getting. If you want to learn more, you can do your own study of how Christ responded to manipulators in the Gospels, or if your parents already have a copy of my book, you can ask them to go over with you what I have written there.

ARE YOU GUILTY OF MISUSING GUILT?

What are your favorite manipulative moves? Look back at the chart covering manipulative motives to help you jog your memory. Do you know what the favorite tactic of those who tried to manipulate Christ was? It was attempting to convict Him of sin that He *did not commit*. In other words, the favorite and perhaps the most effective means of manipulating someone is to try to make him feel guilty.

"Now it came about that on a certain Sabbath He was passing through some grainfields; and His disciples were picking and eating the heads of grain, rubbing them in their hands" (Luke 6:1). On this occasion, the disciples were following Christ through some fields of standing grain. As they were walking, some of the disciples began to strip off some of the grain heads into their hands. At this point, in order to remove the outer bran shell from the inner heart of each grain, they had to first rub the kernels between their hands and then blow just hard enough to scatter the light covering of bran into the air and away from the heavier heart of the kernel. In the eyes of the Pharisees, who held to their traditions more tenaciously than they did to the Bible, this "harvesting" was work and, consequently, unlawful to do on the Sabbath (see Ex. 34:2).

"But some of the Pharisees said, 'Why do you do what is not lawful on the Sabbath?' " (Luke 6:2) Did you catch the "why" question? In asking this question, Jesus' accusers were likely trying to discredit (embarrass) Him, or perhaps were even attempting to affect His conscience with guilt. Regardless of their motive (the text does not provide it), the Pharisees were being manipulative, and Christ wisely detected and responded to their manipulation. (Check it out for yourself.)

Here is another example of the misuse of guilt. The Lord's parents were anxious when they realized that He had not returned from the temple with them to Nazareth. When they found Him three days later "sitting in the midst of the teachers, both listening to them, and asking them questions" (Luke 2:46), "they were astonished" (v. 48), and His mother reproved Him. "Why have you treated us this way? Behold, your father and I have been anxiously looking for you" (v. 48).

Notice the use of questions. Notice the use of the "why" question, clearly used to incite guilt. Notice the sympathetic appeal ("You have hurt us by making us anxious"). Perhaps you've never considered Mary's response to Jesus' behavior to be manipulative. But, whether she did so consciously or unconsciously, to the extent that she tried to make Him feel guilty and/or responsible for her anxiety, technically she was using manipulation.

Now before you start telling yourself that your parents are necessarily being manipulative by asking you "why" questions, let me remind you of two things. First, parents *do* have a right to ask you all kinds of questions—yes, even "why" type questions. "It is . . . the glory of kings [people in positions of authority] to search out a matter" (Prov. 25:2). Second, Mary and Joseph of all people should have known (it was their responsibility to know) that Jesus was the Christ and that God had given Him certain responsibilities that He had to fulfill. They also should have known that Jesus had to be seeing to the affairs of His heavenly Father, not only because of the many Old Testament prophecies written about the ministry of the Messiah, but also because of what Gabriel (Luke 1:26–38), Zacharias (Luke 1:68–79), Simeon (Luke 2:21–35), and Anna the prophetess (Luke 2:36–38) had said concerning Him. More importantly, because He was God and could not sin, trying to convict Him of sin was an exercise in futility.

Another form of manipulating your parents by misusing guilt is making obligatory statements. You should not use sentences that begin with the following phrases without first asking yourself, "Where is it written that my parents are obligated to do that?"

- ☐ You should
- ☐ You can't
- ☐ You must
- ☐ You ought to
- ☐ You've got to

SUPPLICATION VS. MANIPULATION

Since the essence of manipulation is trying to get your parents to give you what you want by evoking some other emotion in their hearts (or sometimes even refusing to come right out and ask them), you will have to change your approach.

Without resorting to forms of communication that pressure your parents to feel guilt (over something that is not sinful), embarrassment, shame, anger, unnecessary pity, or fear, you can simply ask them in clear, concise language to give you what you want (provided, of course, that what you are asking for does not cause anyone to sin).

"Are you saying that I should never tell my parents anything that would cause them to make a decision based on their emotions?"

No. I'm saying that you should *be up front* with them about *what* you want and *why* you want it. If, through your telling them the truth, they feel sympathy for you (because, for example, not to give you what you want might embarrass you), that is fine. What I'm discouraging you from doing is evoking an emotional response without disclosing to them all the necessary information they need to make a wise decision (trying to get them to give you what you want without telling them that you are afraid of being embarrassed).[2]

Let me warn you against asking too hastily—before you have thought through what you are going to say.

The heart of the righteous ponders how to answer. (Prov. 15:28)

The heart of the wise instructs his mouth
And adds persuasiveness to his lips. (Prov. 16:23)

Hastily made requests are often denied. Put yourself in your parents' place. Look at the request from their eyes. More importantly, look at the request from God's point of view. Consider whether He would be pleased to give you what you are requesting. If your parents turn down your request, you should take the denial as from the Lord, knowing that He is working in and through your believing parents. "The king's heart is *like* channels of water in the hand of the LORD; He turns it wherever He wishes" (Prov. 21:1). Even if your parents are not genuine Christians, God still expects you to obey them (unless they ask you to sin). "Children, obey your parents in the Lord, for this is right" (Eph. 6:1).

When you resort to manipulation in order to get something, chances are good that the *something* you want is wrong—not because that something is necessarily sinful in and of itself, but because you want that something (as good as it might be) too much. The fact that you were willing to sin by manipulating your parents for it is proof that you have made an idol of it. Remember, an idolatrous desire is anything I want so much that I'm willing to sin in order to acquire it.

Perhaps your greatest challenge in changing your manipulative approach to getting what you want will be learning how to accept a "no" answer as final (and as from the Lord Himself). How should a Christian teenager look at being denied by a parent something that he really wants? Here are a few options:

2. Of course, being embarrassed is not necessarily a good reason for your parents to change their minds. They may conclude that your embarrassment isn't as important as what they want you to do.

☐ God is able to work in my father's heart to let me have my request.
Since He is the one who can change his heart, I will take my
request to Him and be content with His answer. If, by not taking
"no" for an answer, I displease my heavenly Father who holds
the heart of my earthly father in His hand (Prov. 21:1), He may
delay giving me what I want.

☐ Perhaps I want this request too much. Maybe God wants me to
dethrone this idolatrous desire and seek my happiness in Him
more than in this temporal pleasure.

☐ God asks me to always honor my parents and to obey them unless
they ask me to sin. It is not a sin for them to have denied my
request. If I get angry at them for this, it will not be the right
kind of anger.

☐ God knows not only what I want, but also what I need. If He
doesn't want me to have what I want, it will be best for me not
to have it right now. Maybe He is protecting me from something.
Perhaps He has something better in store for me in the future.

☐ This isn't *only* about me. Perhaps God is trying to teach my parents
something. If I respond graciously to their denial (even if I think
it is unreasonable) and they realize later that they made a wrong
decision, perhaps they will change their approach in granting me
permission to do the things I want to do. But, if I respond sinfully
to their denial, they may not be willing to change their approach,
even if they do realize that they made an error in judgment.

☐ I'm much better off (safer) being in God's will by obeying my
parents than being out of God's will (and in danger) by resisting
their limitation.

☐ Even if my parents make an unwise or unreasonable decision,
God is in the decision and He will use it for my good. God may
be using my folks to do what is best for me, even though they
don't seem to have my best interest at heart.

☐ The Lord is causing all things to work together for my good
(Rom. 8:28–29). I wonder how He intends this "no" to conform
me to the image of Christ.

See how many additional biblical responses to a parental "no" you can come up with on your own.

☐

☐

☐

☐

"All this is fine and good. I'm sure it will help me to do a better job of taking 'no' for an answer. But what if I learn that my parents made their decision based on erroneous information? Or what if I get new relevant information after a decision has been made? Do I still have to live with their decision?"

In the next chapter, I will explain another option you may have at your disposal should you find yourself in such circumstances.

THE APPEAL PROCESS[1]

THE PROCESS OF making an appeal is one of several biblical resources that God has provided to help us defend ourselves from abusive or tyrannical authorities. More importantly, it's an instrument through which a person in a subordinate position may properly influence a person in a position of authority. The kind of appeal that we will consider in this chapter is one that may be utilized once a parental decision has been made.

The Scriptures contain a good number of appeals made by various individuals in different ways for many reasons. Nehemiah appealed to King Artaxerxes that he might rebuild Judah (Neh. 2:1–8). Daniel appealed to his commander so he would not defile himself with King Nebuchadnezzar's food and wine (Dan. 1:8–21). Paul appealed to a higher authority, Caesar, when Festus asked him if he would like to be tried in Jerusalem (Acts 25:6–12). Paul also appealed to a *subordinate*, Philemon, who was himself an authority to Paul's new convert Onesimus (the runaway slave), that he would accept him back and transfer his debt to Paul's own account (Philem. 10–19). Abigail appealed to David not to take his own vengeance on her foolish husband Nabal (1 Sam. 25:18–35). Abraham appealed to the Lord not to destroy Sodom should He find ten righteous inhabitants (Gen. 18:32–33). Judah appealed to

1. This chapter contains concepts that have been adapted and expanded from Gary Ezzo and Anne Marie Ezzo, *Growing Kids God's Way* (Louisiana, MO: Growing Families, 1998).

the second most powerful man in all Egypt (his yet unrevealed brother Joseph) to let Benjamin return to his father Jacob, lest Jacob die of a broken heart (Gen. 44:18–34). Jethro appealed to Moses that he might delegate some of his judicial responsibility to other qualified men (Ex. 18:17–27). David appealed to King Saul to allow him to fight with Goliath (1 Sam. 17:31–37). David later appealed to Saul to stop pursuing (with the intent to kill) him (1 Sam. 26:17–20). Bathsheba, with a bit of prompting from Nathan the prophet, appealed to King David to make Solomon king rather than Adonijah (1 Kings 1:11–27). Moses appealed to the Lord not to destroy His people as He intended (Ex. 32:9–14). Hezekiah appealed to God to extend his life beyond what the Lord originally intended (2 Kings 20:3).

THE APPEAL AND THE LAW OF THE HOUSE

God has given Christian parents the responsibility to develop a set of house rules based on the Scriptures. As we have seen, these rules fall into two distinct categories: "biblically directed rules," which you as a Christian will always be obligated to follow because they are directives commanded by God in Scripture (you may not lie, you may not steal, you may not take your own revenge, and so on) and "biblically derived rules," those that your believing parents develop based on biblical principles in order to facilitate Ephesians 6:4, "And, fathers, do not provoke your children to anger; but bring them up in the discipline and instruction of the Lord." These are house rules that have been *derived* from Scripture and that a Christian ordinarily would *not* be bound to obey. Such a biblically derived house rule might be the following: "Because the Bible says that you must take care of your body (1 Cor. 6:19–20), and it's vain to stay up late and rise early (Ps. 127:2), you may not stay up past 9:30 p.m. on weekdays when you must get up the next morning at 6:00 a.m." However, because such rules have been established by your parents, you are commanded to obey them as long (and only as long) as you are lawfully under their authority.

You may never appeal a biblically directed rule. ("Dad, is it okay if I steal a CD from Walmart? I'm out of money, and the CD is by my favorite Christian artist.") You may appeal a biblically derived rule. ("Dad, there is a special program on television tonight at 9:30 that my teacher suggested we watch. May I break my bedtime 'curfew' to see it?")

The basis of an appeal is the presentation of new or additional data (preferably supported with biblical argument) that you believe your parent has not considered in making a particular decision. You present the new information along with its biblical justification/benefits (i.e., why the Lord might be pleased with a change of mind/decision) to your parents and without any further pressure, thereby allowing them to reevaluate their decision. This process allows your folks to change their minds without having to compromise their parental authority. More importantly, it also trains you to communicate your desires biblically without resorting to disrespect, manipulation, and other manifestations of sinful anger.

HOW TO MAKE AN APPEAL

Biblical appeals, referred to in Scripture by such words as *petitions*, *requests*, and *supplications*, were made in different ways by many individuals depending on the personalities, positions, and circumstances of the individuals involved. The following procedure for making an appeal is one that has been devised for use by teenagers with their parents. It's certainly not the only "right way" of making an appeal. I suggest it as a starting point from which you and your parents may develop and fine-tune a more personalized system:

STEP ONE: The instruction is properly given by the parent.
STEP TWO: The instruction is properly acknowledged by the teen.
STEP THREE: A request for an appeal is properly made by the teen.
STEP FOUR: The appeal is properly acknowledged by the parent.
STEP FIVE: The appeal is made as additional data is presented to the parent by the teen.
STEP SIX: The parent reconsiders his instruction in light of the new information and grants or denies the request.

Step One: The instruction is given by the parent.

A key implication of Ephesians 6:4 is that parents will be giving commands to their children. These commands represent decisions that have (hopefully) been made within the framework of Scripture, but are not necessarily in and of themselves biblical mandates. Most parental decisions and instructions will be of the "biblically derived" variety. Although your parents may not have a particular portion of Scripture in mind when giving instruction, the command may very well be consistent with the "instruction of the Lord" as found in the Bible, with the ultimate aim of developing Christlike character in you.

EXAMPLE: "I want you to be in bed by 9:30 tonight."

Step Two: The instruction is acknowledged by the teen.

At this juncture, you respectfully affirm that you both *understand* and *intend to obey* the instruction, thus placing yourself in the best possible position to make an appeal. This step tends to disarm parents from any unnecessary defensiveness (pride), anger, and fear of being manipulated that might otherwise hinder an objective consideration of your appeal. "The wrath of a king [or an authority; e.g., parents] is as messengers of death, but a wise man will appease it" (Prov. 16:14).

EXAMPLE: "Dad, I understand that you would like me to be in bed by 9:30 tonight (and I intend to do so)."

Step Three: A request for an appeal is made by the teen.

By asking permission to make an appeal (much like Esther did when she presented herself before King Ahasuerus in Est. 5:1–3), you further express humility and submission to authority, communicating that it's your parents' prerogative to grant or deny your request. This further prepares their hearts for objectively considering your appeal. Your choice of wording is very important at this point. You are humbly requesting permission to make an appeal, not questioning or challenging your parents' decision. Acceptable phrases include, "May I appeal?", "Would you permit me to make an appeal?", "May I be allowed to appeal?", or "May I submit an appeal?

EXAMPLE: "I have some new information. May I make an appeal?"

Step Four: The appeal is acknowledged by the parent.

If your parents believe it necessary to hear your appeal, they will do so. If, however, the appeal has not been made correctly (Prov. 26:4), or you have begun to abuse the appeal process, or time will not allow an appeal at that moment, they may decline to hear it.

EXAMPLE (request denied): "I'm not in a particularly appealing mood at this time. Besides, your mother and I have discussed this at length and our decision is final." At this point (sarcasm notwithstanding), the case is closed!

EXAMPLE (request granted): "Yes, you may."

Step Five: The appeal is made as additional data is presented to the parent by the teen.

Additional data is information that you believe your parents should consider—information that you believe they apparently did not consider in making the original decision. It should be *apparent* that the information was not previously considered.

It was apparent to Esther that King Ahasuerus did not know that Esther was a Jew when he gave Haman permission to annihilate the Jews (Est. 2:20; 7:3–4).

It was apparently new information to Philemon that Onesimus had become a Christian through Paul's influence and had begun to minister to him (Philem. 10–11).

Judah apparently perceived that it was new information to Joseph that Benjamin's father loved him so much that he feared for his life should Benjamin not return (Gen. 44:19–32).

It was apparently new information to King Saul that David had killed a wild beast with his own hands (1 Sam. 17:34–36).

"Additional data" includes such things as an expressed conflicting desire of another authority figure (e.g., another parent or a teacher), information that your parent would have no other way of finding out, and biblical arguments for considering another course of action that would better glorify God.

EXAMPLE: "My teacher told us two days ago that a television special about the civil war will be aired tonight at 9:30. She suggested that if we could get permission to watch it, it would help to prepare us for the lesson tomorrow. May I please stay up to watch the program?"

Step Six: The parent reconsiders his instruction in light of the new information and grants or denies the request.

By appealing in this way, your parents can usually evaluate the additional data on its own merit (and in light of the Scriptures) without the distraction of typical concerns such as disrespect or manipulation. Should they grant the appeal, they will do so without feeling pressured into it and without compromising in any way their biblical authority. Should they deny the appeal, they will be better able to explain their reasoning to you without being distracted by your bad attitudes.

EXAMPLE: "Yes, you may watch the program after you have showered, brushed your teeth, and put on your pajamas so that you will be able to go to bed immediately after the special."

EXAMPLE (postponement): "Your mother and I have made other plans tonight that will require our not being distracted. I'd like for you to prepare for bed so that your mother and I will have some time to discuss the matter privately. When you've finished, we will let you know what we've decided."

EXAMPLE: "No, your mother and I made plans to do something else tonight that will require our not being distracted. Had you told one of us about the program when you first learned of it two days ago, we would have made other arrangements. I'm sorry, but I'll have to deny your request."

What I'm about to say is arguably one of the most important principles in this book: as a rule,[2] if you cannot convince your parents to change their minds after *one* well-thought-out, gracious, and respectful appeal, you should consider it to *not be God's will* for you to have your request

2. There may be exceptions to the rule, such as if what your parents are asking you to do is really a sin.

granted at this time. This is the essence of submission to authority. God is able to change your parents' mind. He did not do so, even though you played by His rules and did not resort to sinful means of pressuring your folks to get your way. For you to continue to press the issue at this point by sulking, pouting, begging, whining, or complaining is to try to manipulate your parents into giving you what you want. Do you really think God will bless your sinful efforts to control your parents?

Here is another example of the proper use of the appeal process:

Step One: The instruction is given by the parent.

"Go upstairs and clean your room."

Step Two: The instruction is acknowledged by the teen.

"Yes, ma'am! I realize that my room needs attention immediately..."

Step Three: A request for an appeal is made by the teen.

"But, would you permit me to make an appeal?"

Step Four: The appeal is acknowledged by the parent.

"Go ahead."

Step Five: The appeal is made as additional data is presented to the parent by the teen.

"Last night Dad asked me to wash his pickup today. If I follow your instructions first and attend to my room, by the time I finish, it will be dark. Dad doesn't think I do a good job of washing his car after the sun goes down because I can't see as well. Would it be all right if I washed his car first and then worked on my room?"

Step Six: The parent reconsiders his instruction in light of the new information and grants or denies the request.

"I've got a better idea! You may wash my car and Dad's car now; then after supper, I'll help you clean up your room."

GUIDELINES FOR MAKING AN APPEAL

Here are a few guiding principles to help keep you from abusing the appeal process.

Guideline One: Make every effort to appeal to the parent who is presently giving the instruction.

As a rule, when you are instructed by one parent to do (or not do) something, you should not direct your appeal to the other parent unless it's impossible for you to respond directly to the instructing parent (such as when your father is 32,000 feet in the air, flying to another part of the country on business). To do otherwise would probably be manipulative. It would also be disruptive to parental unity (see Gen. 2:24) and may be contradictory to the principle of parental authority (if your mother, for example, makes a decision that overrules what your father has decided; see Gal. 4:1–2).

Guideline Two: Be sure that your verbal and nonverbal communication reflects both submission to and respect for authority.

Any and all appeals you make should be made using words, tone of voice, and nonverbal communication (the "communication pie" mentioned in chapter 2) that demonstrate parental respect and submission (see Eph. 6:1–2). Thus, appeals that are attempted with manifestations of sinful anger, pouting, sulking, whining, sarcasms, and so on are inappropriate and have a much greater likelihood of being rejected. Such disrespectful and manipulative appeals force your parents to reprimand and even discipline you rather than entertain your appeal.

Guideline Three: Plan on making only one appeal.

By making multiple appeals (e.g., "But, Mom, pleeeeease!" "Why can't I . . . ?" "Well, then, can I . . . ?"), you demonstrate to your folks an unwillingness to graciously accept a "no" answer from them and ultimately from the Lord Himself (see Rom. 13:1–2; Eph. 6:1; Col. 3:20). Let me say it again: if you cannot persuade your parents to reconsider their position after one appeal, you should conclude that "it's apparently not God's will (see 1 Peter 2:13–15) for me to have what I want right now." Knowing that you have only "one opportunity" to approach your parents should motivate you to give the appeal your best effort. That attempt may involve doing any appropriate research beforehand; working on (and even practicing if necessary) the development of the proper wording, tone of voice, and nonverbal communication; and waiting for the best time (like Esther did) to make your request. Hastily made appeals often result in declines, whereas more well-thought-out appeals tend to be more successful. Don't rush things! Slow down and give it your best shot. And, most importantly, be prepared to receive a "no" answer with a good attitude. Remember, your folks may be so used to your attempts at manipulation that they may say no simply from habit. Perhaps when they see that you accept their "no" answer graciously three or four times in a row, they will be more disposed to say yes in the future.

Guideline Four: Consider the appeal process a privilege to be earned rather than a right that cannot be taken away.

The privilege of an appeal comes only to those who have faithfully demonstrated that they can be trusted. Teens whose decisions are characterized by wisdom typically earn the respect necessary to be entrusted with making an appeal. Those who characteristically make foolish choices are probably not trustworthy enough to make appeals in a proper manner (let alone with the proper motives). The Bible warns against placing confidence in unfaithful men (Prov. 12:19). When you abuse the appeal process by making so many appeals that appealing becomes more of a pattern than obedience does, or when you constantly violate any of these four guidelines, you may temporarily lose (be suspended from) appeal privileges.

Every Christian finds himself in subordinate positions at various times in his life. God ordains these relationships. Scripture requires submission by the subordinate to the superior in certain circumstances. Christian wives are to be submissive to their own husbands (see 1 Peter 3:1). Church members are told, "Obey your [church] leaders, and submit to them" (Heb. 13:17). Christian citizens are commanded to be in subjection to the governing authorities (Rom. 13:1), believing slaves (and, by analogy, believing employees) are to be obedient to those who are their masters according to the flesh (and, by analogy, to employers; Eph. 6:5), and, as a general rule, Christians are to "be subject to one another in the fear of Christ" (Eph. 5:21).

Since the ability to make an effective appeal is crucial to any interpersonal relationship involving authority, learning how to appeal to your parents helps to prepare you for lifelong success in such relationships. This character training also teaches you how to implement Colossians 4:6: "Let your speech always be with grace, seasoned, as it were, with salt, *so that you may know how you should respond to each person.*"

Well, there you have it: some Bible basics on how to make an appeal. Please discuss this chapter with your parents to see if they would like to affirm, amend, or tweak the things covered in this chapter. Remember, this approach to making an appeal is derived from Scripture. It's not the only (or necessarily the best) biblical approach to this subject.

13

HOW TO TALK TO YOUR PARENTS ABOUT THEIR SIN

FOR ME, THIS WAS the hardest chapter of the book to write. There is little doubt that the Bible tells you to talk to your believing parents about the sins they regularly commit against you. Teaching you how to do it wisely, respectfully, and carefully is my challenge. Let me say at the outset that I know there will be extenuating circumstances for some of you that will make it impossible to fully follow the advice I'm about to give. Some of you may have parents who profess to be Christians but who act like the Devil. Others may have parents (or a parent) who are unbelievers. Since the scriptural injunctions covered in this book refer to confronting a "brother" (i.e., another Christian), you may be able to apply only a small portion of this chapter to your situation. My suggestion is that you consider sitting down with your parents, asking them to read and discuss this chapter with you, or asking them to read it on their own and then sit down with you to discuss how they would like to see you implement its contents. Another option might be for you to do this with your pastor, youth leader, or another church leader (or biblical counselor) who might be willing to go before you (to be your "John the Baptist" with your folks)—or at least to advise you on the wisdom of implementing this material in your peculiar circumstances.

What follows in this chapter is a set of guiding principles for talking to your parents about the things they do to provoke you to anger. If your folks are truly believers and you approach them correctly, they ought to be willing to listen to you—provided, of course, that you demonstrate to them that you have been willing to get the beam out of your own eye first. So let's begin there.

GUIDELINES FOR TALKING TO YOUR PARENTS ABOUT THEIR SIN

1. Get the beam out of your own eye first.

> Why do you look at the speck that is in your brother's eye, but do not notice the log that is in your own eye? Or how can you say to your brother, "Let me take the speck out of your eye," and behold, the log is in your own eye? You hypocrite, first take the log out of your own eye, and then you will see clearly to take the speck out of your brother's eye. (Matt. 7:3–5)

Your parents should be receptive to this first step whether or not they are believers. Begin by making a list of the ways you have sinned against them and provoked them to anger. Appendix E, "Common Ways in which Teenagers Sin against Their Parents," has been included for this purpose. Please take a quick look at it and then come back.

I know it's a thorough list (all right; it's very long). But remember, I want you to check off only the things that apply to you—especially those things that you do (or don't do) regularly. After you have prayerfully filled out the worksheet, ask your folks if they would be willing to give you their undivided attention (to make an appointment with you) for twenty to thirty minutes (depending on the length of your list). Then sit down with them, read your list to them, and, when you have finished confessing your sins to them, ask their forgiveness *for the entire list*.

Note: I should remind you at this point that if you want the Lord to bless this exercise, your primary motive for doing this must be to please Him. It should not be so that you may get what you want by schmoozing your parents into thinking that you are going to be the ideal teenager from now on. Don't look at this as a gimmick (or it just might backfire on you).

2. Ask your parents for their help.

After you have gained their forgiveness, ask them if they would be willing to do two more things for you. First, ask them to add to the list any other ways in which you have habitually failed (and in which they would like to see you change). Then ask them if they would be willing to put in order of priority the top ten items (from the combined list) on which they would like to see you work to change. They may need a few days to think it through, to confer with each other, and, quite possibly, to get over the shock of your taking the initiative to do this—so please be patient.

Ask your parents to hold you accountable for the areas that they have prioritized. I have even included a weekly Parental Evaluation Form (appendix F), which you may photocopy and use for this purpose. Ask them for suggestions of how you might change and for help with understanding and applying the appropriate passages of Scripture. Perhaps they would be willing to set up a weekly counseling/discipleship session with you. Ask them.

In addition, consider taking the list to one of your church leaders to seek counsel on how you might make the appropriate changes or improvements. Humility begets humility. When your parents see how willing you are to change the patterns of sin in your own life, they just might be more willing than they have ever been in the past to allow you the freedom to talk to them about their sinful behavior.

Before looking at the next few guidelines, allow me first to help you to understand the biblical basis for them. Let's take another look at what Jesus said in Luke 17:3: "Take heed to yourselves. If your brother sins against you, rebuke him; and if he repents, forgive him" (NKJV).

This verse obligates you to go to your sinning brother and "rebuke him." Now the problem is that parents probably won't much appreciate being "rebuked" by their teenage son or daughter. The word *rebuke* itself seems totally antithetical to the idea of showing respect (which, of course, is exactly what the Bible says you must *always* do to your parents). How can a teenager rebuke a parent without being disrespectful? That is the question.

Here is the answer: the word *rebuke* is not the best translation of the original Greek word (at least not in the context of this passage). The word is better translated *convict*—"If your brother sins against you, *convict* him." It's a legal term that embodies the idea of prosecuting a case against another so that he is convicted for the crime that he has committed. It carries with it the idea of refuting an opponent to the point of *convincing* him (or if not him, then at least others who hear the evidence) of his sin. It's substantiating and proving that the charges made against someone are true.

So, you see, there are all sorts of ways to convict someone of his sin while being perfectly polite and respectful. As a counselor, I have to convict people all the time. With some people I have found it effective to use the two-by-four approach. I myself am a two-by-four type of person: "Don't waste your time sugarcoating it. Just tell me what the Bible says (hit me over the head) and get out of my way." (The two-by-four approach is not recommended for parents.) With others I use a much gentler approach. I may simply ask someone a question, which is all that is necessary to bring that person to tears.

After citing Matthew 19:8, I might ask a woman who is contemplating a divorce, "Do you really want to demonstrate to God and to others that you have a hard heart?"

After reading Colossians 3:12, I might ask the father of an angry teen, "Have you ever considered how the harsh tone in your voice might be exasperating your son?"

"Should you really expect God to help you get out of debt when you are working so many hours that it has become all but impossible for you to 'seek first His Kingdom and His righteousness' (Matt. 6:33)?"

At this point you may be asking yourself, "But I thought conviction was the work of the Holy Spirit. What right do I have to try to 'convict' someone—especially my parents?"

The Holy Spirit certainly does convict of sin (John 16:8), as do the Scriptures (2 Tim. 3:16). But God's people are also charged with the ministry of conviction. Paul, for example, commanded Timothy to *convict* those under his spiritual care with the Scriptures. "Preach the word; be ready in season and out of season; reprove [convict], rebuke, exhort, with great patience and instruction" (2 Tim. 4:2). He also told him to *convict* those church leaders "who continue in sin . . . in the presence of all, so that the rest also may be fearful of sinning" (1 Tim. 5:20). In fact, one of the qualifications for being ordained as a pastor in the first place is the ability to convict those who contradict sound doctrine (Titus 1:9). And, in James 2:9–11, the law is used to convict James's hearers of being lawbreakers. Bringing conviction, therefore, is a part of the responsibility of the ministry of the Word.

Of course all three agents of conviction (the Spirit, the Word, and the minister of the Word) are sometimes necessary to bring about the desired result. But when ministering the Word, the human agent must do so under the power of the Holy Spirit for the desired conviction to be effective.

"OK; but, as I said, I'm just a kid. Who am I to convict my parents?"

Don't be so quick to call yourself a kid. I have a surprise for you in the next chapter that *may* cause you to reevaluate that analysis of yourself. But even if you are "just a kid," how does that prohibit you from doing what the Bible says one Christian ought to be lovingly doing to another Christian who is habitually sinning? In my book *Teach Them Diligently*, I wrote about two incidents concerning my eldest daughter.

> I was lying on my bed one afternoon waiting for my wife to finish dressing when she asked me to bring her something she needed. Sophia, our two-year-old daughter, was standing between us as I sighed grudgingly in response to Kim's request for my assistance.
>
> Immediately my little girl, who of course couldn't yet read, said ever so sweetly, "Daddy, you should '*Do all things without complaining or arguing.*'"
>
> Several weeks later (days after her third birthday), the three of us were in a restaurant waiting for our food. The waitress had just brought a coloring place mat and some crayons for Sophia to entertain herself with while our food was being prepared. I was seated across the booth from the girls watching my little artist desecrate the place

mat with her scribblings and scrawlings. At this point, I went into teacher mode. The wise counselor (who should have known that a three-year-old is not developmentally able to do so) began trying to teach his daughter how to color inside the lines. I picked up a crayon and beginning at the top of the paper, I proceeded to color as neatly as I could upside down. Little by little I encroached my way down the sheet until my large paw was crowding out her petite hand. Picture this. My forearm is resting across the entire length of the place mat, my hand is at its bottom, and Sophia has no place to color. At that moment, she looked up and said, "Daddy, the Bible says, '*Do not forget to do good and to <u>share</u>.*'"

Not only did my daughter know the Scriptures at a young age, but she was able to effectively minister them to her college-educated father.

Where is it written that a son or daughter must not confront a sinning parent? If you are a Christian who has believing parents, aren't you obligated to talk to them about their sin according to the Scriptures? I believe that you are.

"Perhaps I am, but I'm not sure of the best way to approach my parents when they sin."

That's why it may be very helpful for you to ask them. First ask them whether they believe it's appropriate for them to talk to you about their sin. Encourage them to read this chapter, and then ask them to give you direction on the best way for you to put it into practice. If they are professing Christians who expect you to behave biblically, they ought to be open to allowing you to use the Bible to discuss their behavior.

3. Be sure that what your parents do to "push your buttons" really is a sin.

You can't confront your parents because they didn't buy you that new Jaguar for your birthday. Luke 17:3 makes it clear that the person you reprove (or convict) must have sinned. You don't convict someone just because he annoys you, upsets you, disappoints you, bursts your bubble, refuses to give you what you want, or makes a decision with which you disagree. He may do any and all of these in the process of sinning, but unless he has clearly sinned, you may not reprove him.[1] Let me remind you of what I said in chapter 5: as much as is possible, you ought to cover (overlook) as many of your folks' sins as you can.

Love covers a multitude of sins. (1 Peter 4:8)

A man's discretion makes him slow to anger,
And it is his glory to overlook a transgression. (Prov. 19:11)

In other words, just as your parents probably don't get on your case about every sin you commit (though I know sometimes it *seems* like they do), so you should not make a federal case about everything that they do wrong. The idea is to cover what you can. It's when another believer continually "throws the covers off" by repeatedly committing the same sin that you must attempt to convict.

4. Examine your motives.

According to Galatians 6:1, the goal you're trying to accomplish when dealing with a brother who is struggling with sin should be restoration. "Brethren, even if a man is caught in any trespass, you who are spiritual, restore such a one in a spirit of gentleness; each one looking to yourself, lest you too be tempted." The word *restore* is a medical term used to describe the setting of a bone that has been broken. The idea is to make a person who has been overpowered by a sin useful again. In other words, your motive for convicting sinning parents should be to restore them—not to expose them, not to make things easier for yourself, not to extract personal vengeance on them by humiliating them, and not to manipulate them into giving you what you want. And you shouldn't try to talk to your parents about their sin when you are sinfully angry—when you are angrier because they have sinned *against you* than because they have sinned *against*

---

1. This is not to imply that you cannot talk to your parents about the nonsinful things that they do to bug you. It's only to say that your motive and approach for discussing those things are going to be other than conviction.

God. This, in part, is what Paul meant when he added the words "in a spirit of gentleness; each one looking to yourself, lest you too be tempted" to those he had charged with this restorative injunction. Jesus used the word "hypocrite" to describe those who don't examine their own "log" before speaking to another about his "speck" (see Matt. 7:3–5). Think about how you felt when your parents spoke to you about your issues in an angry, harsh, condescending way. How easy was it for you to take that kind of criticism?

5. Use biblical terminology when talking to your parents about their sins.

Follow the example of Paul, who spoke "not in words taught us by human wisdom but in words taught by the Spirit, expressing spiritual truths in spiritual words" (1 Cor. 2:13 NIV). To tell your mother that she is "paranoid" will tempt her to anger sooner than it will bring conviction. To target her conscience (which is where conviction takes place), if you are certain that you have done nothing to cause her to distrust you,[2] you will do better to utilize biblical terms (politely *asking* her, for example, to consider whether she is being inordinately *fearful* or *suspicious*). Telling your father that he is being pigheaded is not, as a rule, nearly as effective as politely telling him that he does not seem open to reason (see James 3:17 ESV; or in the KJV, that he is not "easy to be intreated").

"But I'm not sure that I know the Bible well enough to do this."

Then get hold of a concordance and learn how to use it! You can't effectively confront your parents with their sin without knowing and using the Bible. It's not that you will always have to cite chapter and verse to them. In most cases, just using the appropriate biblical terminology will be sufficient to help them realize that they really have sinned. But since the Spirit of God brings conviction through the Word of God, you really have little hope of convicting them apart from it.

---

2. I cannot emphasize enough that you must be sure to get the beam out of your own eye *before* you attempt to speak to your parents about their sin. To be doubly sure, after examining your own actions, you may want to ask them whether you have provoked the very sin of which you are planning to convict them.

6. Choose the right time.

King Solomon gave us an important insight that can be properly applied to the timing of talking to your parents about all important matters. In Ecclesiastes 3:7 he reminds us that there is "a time to be silent, and a time to speak." The best time to discuss these issues with your folks is when you can secure their undivided attention, which, of course, you may have to ask for explicitly—possibly setting up a specific time in advance. The last thing you will want to do is to talk to them about their sin while they are talking to you about yours—at least not without first taking the hit for (thoroughly acknowledging, repenting, and asking forgiveness for) what you have done wrong. Jesus said, "Come to terms quickly with your accuser" (Matt. 5:25 ESV). Don't even think about trying to convict your folks until after you have come to terms with them. It's often best to wait for a subsequent conversation to bring up their sin. "Why?" you ask. Consider my next point.

7. Choose the right words.

"The heart of the righteous ponders how to answer" (Prov. 15:28). It's often necessary to invest extra time, effort, and thought when selecting just the right words you will use to express to your parents how they have sinned. Then you must be sure that the tone of your voice and your nonverbal communication are entirely humble, gentle, and respectful—not condescending, arrogant, or sarcastic. Perhaps the most difficult thing will be for you to determine the posture you will take as you try to discuss these matters with them. ("I rebuke you in the name of Jesus" will not get you very far.) You must take care not to be too familiar with your folks. Do not treat them like a peer, but treat them with the esteem that they deserve as your parents. You will want to go as a servant and a learner, realizing that they possess more wisdom (as a rule) and life experience than you do and that you may be wrong in your analysis. Even as you are trying to persuade them, let them know that you are open to the fact that you may be wrong. Be careful also not to use the sinful forms of communication that we looked at in chapter 3.

Once again, it's best to discuss "how to do this convicting thing" with your parents before you attempt to do it. Let them "put the words in your mouth." Role-play a few scenarios with them. "Mom, how would you like me to approach you when I think you are showing partiality to my brother?" "Dad, how may I best bring it to your attention when I truly think you are being harsh and unreasonable with me?"

8. Be sure you maintain a gentle spirit throughout the discussion (Gal. 6:1).

Paul warns us to go "in a spirit of gentleness." As we saw in chapter 5, the word *meekness* (or *gentleness*) combines the elements of being *humble* with being *slow to anger*. When your parents sin against you, it may evoke righteous indignation in your heart. It's essential, however, that you do not express your holy passion with sinful forms of communication. Perhaps one of the best ways to keep this from happening is to realize that they have sinned against *God* more than they have sinned against you. The trick is to take yourself out of the picture long enough to look at their sin from His perspective. If you truly love God, you will be more concerned about helping your parents to get back on track (restoring them) than you will be about getting them to stop making life so miserable for you by their sin. If you are too angry, it may simply be because, at that moment, you love yourself more than you love God and your (closest) neighbor.

When your parents sin, seek to avoid the two sinful extremes of blowing up and clamming up that we looked at in chapter 2. Instead, look for a biblical way to attack the problem through biblical means of communication.

Do you remember the Parental Provocation Worksheet (appendix C) that I asked you to fill out at the end of chapter 6? Do you remember that second option I promised you? Here it is. Now may be a good time for you to go over the worksheet with your parents, following the guidelines we discussed in this chapter. Don't forget to point out to them the things you have learned about the sinfulness of your own heart, the biblical resources you have discovered as a result of reading this book, and how you intend to change the way you respond to their provocations.

14

WHAT DOES IT MEAN TO BE A TEEN?

I TOLD YOU that I had a surprise for you in this final chapter. Actually, it might be more of a shock! It has to do with the extent to which you should be treated as an adult.

Did you know that down through the ages, people were considered to be adults at a much younger age than we consider them to be today? In the Hebrew culture, for example, young people went through a "right of passage" called a *bar mitzvah* (for young men) and a *bat mitzvah* (for young women).[1] This was a celebration that meant the individual had transitioned from childhood to adulthood. From this point forward, the parent could no longer be held liable for his child's dishonorable moral or religious behavior. (This was considered a great cause of rejoicing!) The young person would now be considered an adult and would increasingly be given more adult responsibilities. At what age did this "right of passage" occur? Young men typically had their bar mitzvahs at the age of thirteen. Young women could "graduate" at the age of twelve.

Historians have found significant documentation that many other civilizations had similar "right of passage" celebrations. In fact, many scholars are convinced that the long gap between childhood and adulthood, which we call adolescence, simply didn't exist in ancient cultures.

1. This "right of passage" still goes on today in the Jewish community.

It seems that up until the late 1800s or so, young people all around the world between the ages of twelve and sixteen were considered old enough to marry, go to war, vote, and do numerous other things that our culture believes teenagers to be too immature to handle. Of course, these cultures presumably did a much better job of preparing them to do so at a younger age than ours does.[2]

Ronald Koteskey, for example, in his book *Understanding Adolescence*, gives us the legal marrying ages in ancient Rome, merry old England, and early America:

> Two thousand years ago under Roman law, women could marry at twelve and men at fourteen. A thousand years ago under English law, it was the same. Two hundred years ago under common law in the United States, it was still the same—women could marry at twelve and men at fourteen. For 3000 years, the minimum legal age for marriage did not change. Of course, not everyone married at twelve or fourteen, just as everyone does not marry at eighteen today.[3]

Koteskey makes the case that adolescence as we know it (i.e., a protracted six- to seven-year period of time in a young adult's life in which he or she is still considered to be a child) is a man-made and relatively new idea.

> Historian John Demos of Brandeis University and Virginia Demos in the Program of Human Development at Harvard University put it this way: "The concept of adolescence, as generally understood and applied, did not exist before the last two decades of the nineteenth century. One could almost call it an invention of that period."[4]

> In the journal of the American Academy of Arts and Sciences, David Bakan said, "The idea of adolescence as an intermediary period of life

---

2. It's not that there wasn't a learning curve for these ancient teens. It just wasn't as large as it is for today's teens. Their civilizations did not require as much in the way of preparation as ours does.

3. Ronald Koteskey, *Understanding Adolescence* (Wheaton, IL: Victor Books, 1987), 9–10.

4. Ibid., 11, quoting John Demos and Virginia Demos, "Adolescence in Historical Perspective," *Journal of Marriage and the Family* 31, no. 4 (November 1969): 632.

starting at puberty . . . is the product of modern times. . . . [It developed] in the latter half of the nineteenth and the early twentieth century . . . to prolong the years of childhood."[5]

We did not just coin a new word to describe something that had always existed. We did just the opposite. We took an old word and used it to mean something that we had just created. *Adolescence* now refers to the teen years, during which we treat people as children even though they are adults. It is not a matter of what we call teenagers; it is how we treat them.[6]

The Bible doesn't isolate the teenage years as a special period of time in a person's life. Nor does it indicate that teenagers should be treated as anything other than adults. (Of course, a parent may be compelled by Scripture to treat and admonish a spiritually immature or irresponsible teenager as a child until such time as the teen demonstrates that he should be treated otherwise.)[7] It doesn't say anything about this protracted period of time (the gap) called *adolescence*. In fact, in several places, the Bible supports the idea of a quick transition from childhood to adulthood. Notice, for example, the quick transitional language from childhood to adulthood in the life of Moses.

> The *child* grew, and she brought him to Pharaoh's daughter, and he became her son. And she named him Moses, and said, "Because I drew him out of the water."
> Now it came about in those days, *when Moses had grown up*, that he went out to his brethren and looked on their hard labors; and he saw an Egyptian beating a Hebrew, one of his brethren. (Ex. 2:10–11)

There is no hint of adolescence in this passage.

"But Moses wrote the book of Exodus. Maybe he purposely left stuff out about his teenage years because he was ashamed of what he did."

5. Ibid., quoting David Bakan, "Adolescence in America: From Idea to Social Fact," *Daedalus* 100, no. 4 (Fall 1971): 979–95.
6. Ibid.
7. See Proverbs 12:19; 26:1, 8; Matthew 25:14–29; Luke 16:12; 19:13–26; 1 Corinthians 3:1–3.

Well, the writer of the book of Hebrews records things pretty much the same way—from childhood to adulthood with no mention of adolescence.

> By faith Moses, when he was born, was hidden for three months by his parents, because they saw he was a beautiful *child*; and they were not afraid of the king's edict. By faith Moses, *when he had grown up*, refused to be called the son of Pharaoh's daughter. (Heb. 11:23–24)

And then there are the words of John, who identifies four types of people (little children, children, young men, and fathers), none of which involve the modern notion of adolescence.

> I am writing to you, *little children*, because your sins have been forgiven you for His name's sake. I am writing to you, *fathers*, because you know Him who has been from the beginning. I am writing to you, *young men*, because you have overcome the evil one. I have written to you, *children*, because you know the Father. I have written to you, *fathers*, because you know Him who has been from the beginning. I have written to you, *young men*, because you are strong, and the word of God abides in you, and you have overcome the evil one. (1 John 2:12–14)

John uses another interesting phrase in his gospel that clearly indicates that young people reach a point in their lives when they are to be considered adults.[8]

> The Jews then did not believe it of him, that he had been blind and had received sight, until they called the parents of the very one who had received his sight, and questioned them, saying, "Is this your son, who you say was born blind? Then how does he now see?" His parents answered them and said, 'We know that this is our son, and

8. The Bible doesn't tell us what this age is. That is probably because it's not the same for everyone. My belief is that it should be left up to the father to determine. Notice who makes the call about such things in this passage. "Now I say, as long as the heir is a child, he does not differ at all from a slave although he is owner of everything, but he is under guardians and managers until the date set by the father" (Gal. 4:1–2).

that he was born blind; but how he now sees, we do not know; or who opened his eyes, we do not know. Ask him; *he is of age*, he will speak for himself." His parents said this because they were afraid of the Jews; for the Jews had already agreed that if anyone confessed Him to be Christ, he was to be put out of the synagogue. For this reason his parents said, "*He is of age*; ask him." (John 9:18–23)

Jesus was a teenager, to be sure.[9] But He wasn't an adolescent. At the age of twelve, He was sitting in the synagogue astonishing those who heard Him (see Luke 2:47).[10] His mother Mary was chosen by God while she was a teen to carry, deliver, and care for the Lord Jesus. David slew Goliath as a teen. Daniel, as a teenager, "made up his mind that he would not defile himself with the king's choice food or with the wine which he drank; so he sought permission from the commander of the officials that he might not defile himself" (Dan. 1:8). And let's not forget his three faithful and courageous friends who were also led off to captivity as teens: Shadrach, Meshach, and Abednego. Here are a few more notable teenagers from the Bible whom you may have missed.

And *Ishmael . . . was thirteen* years old when he was circumcised. (Gen. 17:25)

All the people of Judah took *Azariah*, who was *sixteen* years old, and made him king in the place of his father Amaziah. (2 Kings 14:21)

Uzziah was *sixteen* years old when he became king, and he reigned fifty-two years in Jerusalem. . . . He did right in the sight of the LORD according to all that his father Amaziah had done. (2 Chron. 26:3–4)

Jehoiachin was *eighteen* years old when he became king, and he reigned three months in Jerusalem. . . . He did evil in the sight of the LORD, according to all that his father had done. (2 Kings 24:8-9).

9. Actually, the word *teenager* didn't appear in print until the first half of the twentieth century.
10. They were not astonished *that* a twelve-year-old was sitting in the synagogue asking questions, but were astonished at the *kind* of questions this twelve-year-old was asking.

And there was a *young man* [probably a teen] named *Eutychus* sitting on the window sill, sinking into a deep sleep; and as Paul kept on talking, he was overcome by sleep and fell down from the third floor and was picked up dead. (Acts 20:9)

And let's not lose sight of Joseph (Jacob's son), Josiah, Ruth, Isaiah, Jeremiah, Hezekiah, Joseph (Mary's husband), and (John) Mark, who all made appearances in the Bible as teens.

Now, I'm not saying that the old way is necessarily better than the modern way or that we should necessarily go back to the way things used to be. There are definite benefits to the way our society does things. For example:

It's *good* that our culture protects children and young adults from all kinds of abuse. It was the desire to protect children from abuse—especially in the work place—that largely drove this transition.[11]

It's *good* that parents get to enjoy having their children at home for a few more years.

It's *good* that this additional time at home gives parents additional opportunities to influence their children for good.

The point I'm trying to make by questioning the validity of the modern construct of adolescence is that our society may be doing our teenagers a disservice by treating them as if they are not fully responsible. Accepting the world's construct of adolescence lowers the expectations of both parent and teen below those of Scripture. If God believes teenagers are capable not only of behaving maturely but also of serving Him faithfully by ministering to others, what right do we have to believe any less?

College pastor Rick Holland sheds more light on the dilemma.

We are not too different from Saul and the rest of the men of Israel who looked at a young teen named David as an insignificant youth

---

11. Other things that contributed to the development of the American adolescent construct were (1) the establishment of compulsory education, (2) the establishment of a juvenile justice system, and (3) the proliferation of popular psychology, whose theories were developed without (and in opposition to) biblical truth.

(see I Sam. 17:33 and context) just before he leveled Goliath. If God put such stock in a "youth," why don't we?

By creating this mythical state known as adolescence the teenager is in constant flux between childhood and adulthood since he is not fully accepted as either. This is a significant part of the teen problems in our society. It contributes greatly to the teen syndrome of seeking identity in peer groups, gangs, drugs, alcohol, and premarital sex. It also generates anger at parents and a general anti-establishment attitude. The problem is that in some contexts, the young person is patronized as a child, yet in others he is expected to act responsibly as an adult. And we wonder why teens are so confused![12]

I believe teens should be given the opportunity to prove themselves to be responsible adults and, as much as is possible, to be treated as such. It's my view that during those years that society calls *adolescence*, the relationship between parent and teen should be increasingly characterized by friendship and decreasingly characterized by authority and subordination. The following will explain why.

WHAT IT MEANS TO LEAVE AND CLEAVE

God created most of us so that we would be lonely without the company of a lifetime companion to enjoy. He instituted a "covenant of companionship" called marriage. "For this cause a man shall leave his father and his mother, and shall cleave to his wife; and they shall become one flesh" (Gen. 2:24).

The idea is that someday children are to leave their parents to establish a new decision-making unit (a family). The word *leave* is a very strong word in both the original Hebrew and the Greek. It's sometimes translated as *abandon* and *forsake*. We actually came across it in chapter 4 when we looked at Proverbs 28:13: "He who conceals his transgressions will not prosper, but he who confesses and *forsakes* them will find

12. Rick Holland, "The Myth Called Adolescence," *Voice: An Independent Church Journal* (July–August 2002): 9. Rick Holland is the staff elder and director of student ministries, as well as the college pastor, at Grace Community Church in Sun Valley, California. He has served in youth ministry for 21 years and teaches as adjunct professor of youth ministries at the Master's College.

compassion." The Hebrew word *azab* has significant implications for "leaving" one's parent. What is it that children leave behind when they get married?[13]

Getting married means leaving behind parental authority.

Although you must always honor your parents, your responsibility to obey them ends when you become a part of the new decision-making unit.

Getting married means leaving behind parental provision.

When you marry, you will sever your emotional and financial ties to your parents. Your emotional umbilical cord will be cut and reconnected to your spouse. No longer will your parents be your first line of counsel and encouragement. Instead of depending on them for financial support, you and your spouse will look directly to the Lord for provision—and then to each other.

Getting married means leaving behind adherence to those parental lifestyles, beliefs, values, and dispensations that are not clearly delineated in the Scriptures.

Your parents have their own unique lifestyle (way of living). Perhaps they buy their clothes at Neiman Marcus and Brooks Brothers. Perhaps they drive a Mercedes Benz, are members of a country club, and eat out at fancy restaurants three times a week. Maybe they own a cabin in the mountains or a second home at the beach. Or perhaps they do most of their shopping at Walmart, drive a jalopy, couldn't find the local country club with a map, and struggle to keep up the payments on their home that is on the poor side of town. A person may live either of these lifestyles without violating Scripture. When you get married, you may choose to live a more traditional lifestyle than your parents or a more "yuppie" lifestyle. As long as the lifestyle you opt for does not veer outside of biblical parameters, you can choose whatever one you

---

13. I'm grateful to Dr. Wayne Mack, who first taught me these implications of Genesis 2:24.

like. The same is true for many of the things that you value, believe, and establish as house rules (dispensations) for your children. Essentially, you are not obligated to take anything from your parents' marriage *that is not clearly spelled out in the Bible* into your own.[14]

Now, the reason I say that the relationship between parent and teen during the "adolescent years" should increasingly be characterized by friendship and decreasingly characterized by authority and subordination is to prepare all parties for the new adult relationship—friendship, really—that is right around the corner. As we have seen, when you get married, your relationship with your parents is going to change drastically.

It shouldn't deteriorate but should take on the characteristics of friendship (mature brothers and sisters in Christ). Since this is the way things are (hopefully) going to be someday, now is the time for both parent and child to start preparing and practicing for that kind of relationship. Of course, all this is going to be largely dependent upon your level of maturity. You are really the one in the driver's seat.

WHAT DOES THIS ALL MEAN?

It means that the more responsible you are, the more likely your parents will be to treat you as an adult. The more irresponsible you are, the more likely they will be forced to treat you as a child. But you are the one who most influences the way your parents see you. How do you see yourself? Would you say that you perceive yourself more as a child or more as an adult? Are you mature or immature? Think in terms of spiritual maturity. Are you really mature from God's perspective? Your parents are not likely to see you (let alone treat you) as more mature than you see yourself.

Now I know that you probably want to be treated more like an adult than like a child—but put yourself in your parents' place. Are you giving them reason to treat you with the adult prerogatives, privileges, and responsibilities for which you long? Or are you teaching them to

14. Of course, there are probably many of these things from both sets of parents that you and your future spouse will *agree together* to incorporate into your marriage.

treat you as a child by the way you behave? You see, the independence you want will be granted in direct proportion to the degree that your parents trust you. You are, in one sense, their trainer. You train them to trust you or distrust you. Twenty-four hours a day you are instructing them as to whether or not you can be trusted. They will determine how much you can be trusted by observing the way you make decisions.[15]

As your folks see you make wise decision after wise decision about major life issues (like the diligence with which you approach your schooling, the kind of friends you choose, the appropriateness of the entertainment you prefer) with relatively few foolish decisions, they will be more disposed to trust you.

On the other hand, if your parents see you make foolish decision after foolish decision, they will most likely conclude that you cannot be trusted. And, to the degree that they don't trust you, you forfeit the privileges and responsibilities of adulthood.

You see, your parents want you to succeed in life. So they have two basic choices. Their first choice is to do everything they can to help you succeed—to push you forward. If they don't believe that you are mature enough, they default to the second choice: to prevent you from failing—to hold you back. This means more parental control (management) over your life because, in their minds, you don't have enough *self*-control to manage your own life. Bottom line: you lose freedom.

FAITHFULNESS IS THE KEY

Here is a biblical principle that, if learned as a teen, will serve you well throughout the rest of your life. It's the principle of faithfulness. You have probably read the word *faithful* in your Bible dozens of times. Do you know what it means? To be faithful is to be dependable, trustworthy, and reliable. It means that people can count on you to do what you say you are going to do, that they can entrust you with a responsibility and be assured that you will properly fulfill that responsibility. Faithfulness is demonstrating to God and to others that you can be trusted with

15. I'm indebted to Christian author Buddy Scott, who many years ago introduced me to the basic concepts discussed in this section.

more and more responsibility based on your past performance (i.e., the steadfast execution of your previous responsibilities).

This principle of faithfulness can be seen in the parable of the talents recorded in Matthew 25:14–30. You remember the story. A man who is about to go on a journey calls three of his slaves and entrusts his possessions to them (he gives them each a responsibility). To one he gives five talents,[16] to another two talents, and to the third one a single talent ("each according to his own ability," v. 15). Then he goes away, and his slaves go to work investing the money. Well, actually, two of them do. The third slave simply digs a hole, buries the talent, and waits for his master to return.

When the master comes back after a long time to "settle accounts" with his slaves (to hold them accountable), he finds that the first two slaves have doubled his money. To each of them he says, "Well done, good and *faithful* slave; you were faithful with a few things, I will put you in charge of many things; enter into the joy of your master" (vv. 21, 23).

But to the third, he says, "You wicked, *lazy* slave, you knew that I reap where I did not sow, and gather where I scattered no seed. Then you ought to have put my money in the bank, and on my arrival I would have received my money back with interest" (vv. 26–27).

From this parable we can see three elements of faithfulness: *responsibility* (the slaves were entrusted with a task), *accountability* (the master "settled accounts" with them, v. 19), and *reward* (all three men were rewarded according to their faithfulness—or lack of it).

So it is with you. You are given a task (a responsibility) by your parents. After a period of time, you are held accountable (you give an account of how you fulfilled the responsibility). You are then rewarded according to your faithfulness.

Another interesting thing to note in our parable is that part of the reward involved additional responsibilities. "I will put you in charge of many things," the master said to the two faithful slaves. Do you remember what he did to the responsibilities of the lazy slave? He took them away:

16. It's hard to say exactly how much a talent would be worth in today's economy. It was a large sum of money—more than most people would have made in several years back then.

Therefore take away the talent from him, and give it to the one who has the ten talents. For to everyone who has, more shall be given, and he will have an abundance; but from the one who does not have, even what he does have shall be taken away. (vv. 28–29)

The following diagram illustrates a person's progression up the stairs of faithfulness. Notice that with each reward a new level of *responsibility* comes, for which there will be another time of *accountability* and another level of *reward*, as the individual moves up the stairway to ever-increasing faithfulness.

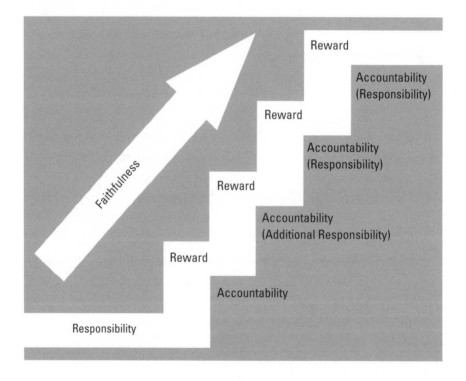

"I've got it. But what does all this have to do with anger management?" you may be wondering.

Simply this. If you are not seriously cooperating with the Holy Spirit's desire for you to develop gentleness (the antithesis of sinful anger), your immaturity in this area will continue to significantly hinder the amount of trust (and consequently freedom) that your parents will give you. Your relationship with your parents might stay "stuck" at this level for years to come. And, if you are an angry person, all your friendships will be adversely affected (see Prov. 22:24–25).

As we bring this "crash course in biblical anger management for teenagers" to a close, let me direct you to a portion of Scripture that follows the last recorded episode of Christ's life as a youth.

> And He said to them, "Why is it that you were looking for Me? Did you not know that I had to be in My Father's house?" But they did not understand the statement which He had made to them. And He went down with them and came to Nazareth, and *He continued in subjection to them*; and His mother treasured all these things in her heart. *And Jesus kept increasing in wisdom and stature, and in favor with God and men.* (Luke 2:49–52)

Isn't this interesting? Here we have the Lord Jesus at the ripe old age of twelve *convicting* both of his parents for not knowing and applying the Scriptures that pertain to Him, and yet "continuing in subjection to them." If ever a teenager were mature and had the right to tell his parents not to get into His space, it was Jesus. But He didn't! He understood, even as a teen, that it was not yet time for Him to cut the cord. So He continued to submit Himself to their authority.

In that state of submission young Jesus continued to grow. He grew *in wisdom*: He grew in His knowledge of how to apply the Scriptures to the new situations that He faced. He grew *in stature*: He filled out, bulked up, and grew taller. He grew *in favor with God*: He grew in His understanding of how to do those things that are pleasing to God. And He grew *in favor with men*: He grew socially, increasing in His ability to interact with adults as an adult. This is my prayer for you.

May you continue to mature in your walk with Christ—no longer as a child, but in dependence upon the Holy Spirit, learning how to speak the truth in love, *growing up in every way* into Him who is the head, into Christ.

Appendix A

HOW TO BECOME A CHRISTIAN

THE NEXT FEW pages contain information that could impact your life more profoundly than anything else you have learned in this book. Please read them carefully.

Many people believe that getting to heaven is accomplished by doing good things and relatively few bad things. The truth, however, is that even one sin is enough to keep you out of heaven. It really doesn't matter how much good you do; any sin—regardless of how great or small—is enough to keep you out of heaven and to send you straight to hell.

> For the wages of sin is death, but the free gift of God is eternal life in Christ Jesus our Lord. (Rom. 6:23)

> For whoever keeps the whole law and yet stumbles in one point, he has become guilty of all. For He who said, "Do not commit adultery," also said, "Do not commit murder." Now if you do not commit adultery, but do commit murder, you have become a transgressor of the law. (James 2:10–11)

> Through one man sin entered into the world, and death through sin, and so death spread to all men, because all sinned. (Rom. 5:12)

According to the Bible, for a person to be saved and go to heaven, there must first be the realization that his sin has caused a separation

215

from God. God, who is both holy and just, must deal with sinners and their sin appropriately. God's holiness disposes Him to hate sin. His justice requires Him to punish sin. The wages or punishment of sin is death (see Gen. 2:17; Rom. 5:12; 6:23). For Him to simply overlook sin without requiring the proper punishment would go against His holy and just nature.

How just would you consider a judge to be if, out of partiality to a convicted serial murderer, he sentenced him only to a few days in jail rather than to at least the minimum sentence required by the law?

Well, what kind of magistrate would God, "the Judge of all the earth" (Gen. 18:25), be if He didn't punish sinners who transgress His law? For God to let sinners off the hook without demanding that they pay at least the minimum penalty for their crimes would render Him unjust (and unfit for the bench). Since the minimum sentence for sin, according to the Bible, is death, God must punish sinners. His justice requires Him to do so.

> It is appointed for men to die once and after this comes judgment. (Heb. 9:27)

> The Lord knows how to rescue the godly from temptation, and to keep the unrighteous under punishment for the day of judgment. (2 Peter 2:9)

> And I saw a great white throne and Him who sat upon it, from whose presence earth and heaven fled away, and no place was found for them. And I saw the dead, the great and the small, standing before the throne, and books were opened; and another book was opened, which is the book of life; and the dead were judged from the things which were written in the books, according to their deeds. And the sea gave up the dead which were in it, and death and Hades gave up the dead which were in them; and they were judged, every one of them according to their deeds. And death and Hades were thrown into the lake of fire. This is the second death, the lake of fire. (Rev. 20:11–14)

Now, there are other elements of God's nature that dispose Him to be loving and merciful. In fact, the Bible says that God is "not willing that any should perish but that all should come to repentance" (2 Peter 3:9 NKJV).

"But how can He forgive sinners in love and mercy when His justice requires Him to punish them for their sins?"

God had to find a substitute—someone who was willing to pay the penalty in the place of sinners.

> Men of Israel, listen to these words: Jesus the Nazarene, a man attested to you by God with miracles and wonders and signs which God performed through Him in your midst, just as you yourselves know—this Man, delivered up by the predetermined plan and foreknowledge of God, you nailed to a cross by the hands of godless men and put Him to death. And God raised Him up again, putting an end to the agony of death, since it was impossible for Him to be held in its power. (Acts 2:22–24)

If God could find someone who was willing to pay the price for men's sin but who did not have to die for his own sin, He could punish that substitute in the sinner's place. But who is without sin? Only God. So God, in His love and mercy, took upon Himself the form of a man in the person of Jesus Christ (Phil. 2:7). The Lord Jesus lived a sinless life and then sacrificed Himself on the cross as the substitute for sinners who were incapable of redeeming themselves. After He was buried He rose from the dead, and in so doing demonstrated His power over death and sin and hell. "For Christ also died for sins once for all, the just for the unjust, in order that He might bring us to God, having been put to death in the flesh, but made alive in the spirit" (1 Peter 3:18).

This resurrection power is available to those who are truly willing to let go of their sins and to believe the gospel (the good news about what Christ did by dying on the cross). The gospel of Jesus Christ provides them power not only over death and hell, but also over sin—the very sin that has enslaved them and caused them so much misery.

Have you ever turned away from your sin and asked God to forgive you once and for all on the basis of Christ's substitutionary death on the cross?

> If you confess with your mouth Jesus as Lord, and believe in your heart that God raised Him from the dead, you shall be saved; for with the heart man believes, resulting in righteousness, and with the mouth he confesses, resulting in salvation. . . . For "Whoever will call upon the Name of the Lord will be saved." (Rom. 10:9–10, 13)

> For God so loved the world, that He gave His only begotten Son, that whoever believes in Him shall not perish, but have eternal life. . . .
> He who believes in the Son has eternal life; but he who does not obey the Son shall not see life, but the wrath of God abides on him. (John 3:16, 36)

When a person becomes a Christian, the Holy Spirit indwells him (takes up residency inside him), giving him the power to obey God. Your ability to make use of the biblical resources contained in this book will be severely limited if you do not have the Spirit's enabling power in your life. He is the true Comforter. He can come alongside you and assist you in your efforts not only to deal with your anger, but also to live the kind of life that is pleasing to Him.

> Therefore, having been justified by faith, we have peace with God through our Lord Jesus Christ, through whom also we have access by faith into this grace in which we stand, and rejoice in hope of the glory of God. And not only that, but we also glory in tribulations, knowing that tribulation produces perseverance; and perseverance, character; and character, hope. Now hope does not disappoint, because the love of God has been poured out in our hearts by the Holy Spirit who was given to us. For when we were still without strength, in due time Christ died for the ungodly. For scarcely for a righteous man will one die; yet perhaps for a good man someone would even dare to die. But God demonstrates His own love toward us, in that while we were still sinners, Christ died for us. (Rom. 5:1–8 NKJV)

Appendix B

HOW TO RESPOND TO REPROOF[1]

Do not reprove a scoffer, or he will hate you,
Reprove a wise man and he will love you. (Prov. 9:8 NASB)[2]

AS YOU READ through this appendix, please try to keep in mind that your believing parents have a double duty to reprove you—first, because you are their child (see Heb. 12: 5–11), and second, because you are a Christian (see Luke 17:3).

Few people realize the abundance of instruction contained in Scripture about responses to reproof. Even fewer seem to possess the humility and discipline necessary to develop the skills to make use of the instruction. Let's begin by looking at some of the sinful responses to reproof.

Despising Reproof: "[They] would have none of my counsel and despised all my reproof." (Prov. 1:30 ESV)

Rejecting Reproof: "Whoever heeds instruction is on the path to life, but he who rejects reproof leads others astray." (Prov. 10:17 ESV)

1. The material in this appendix has been adapted from my article entitled "A Biblical Alternative to Criticism," which first appeared in the *Journal of Pastoral Practice* 10, no. 4 (1992), 15–25.

2. Unless otherwise noted, the Scripture references in this appendix are from the New King James Version of the Bible.

Hating Reproof: "Whoever loves discipline loves knowledge, but he who hates reproof is stupid." (Prov. 12:1 ESV)

If we do not train our ears to hear God's reproofs, we run the risk of responding incorrectly. Examine the following unbiblical but all-too-common approaches to reproof. To how many of them have you resorted in recent weeks? (Please keep your parents' reproofs in mind.)

1. Assuming that, since your reprover had his own personal deficiencies, God will not use him to point out your deficiencies.

In 1 Kings 13, we read of an unnamed prophet who was commanded by God to ride into Bethel and deliver a message to King Jeroboam, and he was given a rather unusual instruction: "You shall not eat bread, nor drink water, nor return by the same way you came" (v. 9). When the prophet delivered the message to Jeroboam, the king raised his hand to have the prophet seized, but immediately his extended hand dried up so that the king couldn't bring it back to his side. At this point Jeroboam had a change of heart and pled, "Please entreat the favor of the LORD your God, and pray for me, that my hand may be restored to me" (v. 6). Jeroboam then invited the prophet to his home for some refreshment and a reward. "If you were to give me half your house, I would not go in with you; nor would I eat bread nor drink water in this place. For so it was commanded me by the word of the LORD, saying, 'You shall not eat bread, nor drink water, nor return by the same way you came' " (vv. 8–9).

On his way back, the man of God stopped to rest under an oak tree. There another, older prophet, who had heard what happened in Bethel, sought the man of God and invited him home for a meal. The invitation was declined by the same statement, but the older prophet was more persistent: "I too am a prophet as you are, and an angel spoke to me by the word of the LORD, saying, 'Bring him back with you to your house, that he may eat bread and drink water' " (v. 18). But, the text continues, "He was lying to him" (v. 18 NIV).

Think about that. Here is a man of God lying to another man of God with a lie that misrepresented God Himself—a deliberate, premeditated, blatant deception that was designed to contradict the word of God and lead another man into disobedience. Do you think that God would resort to using such a scoundrel to communicate a rebuke? Let's see.

> Now it happened, as they sat at the table, that the word of the LORD came to the prophet who had brought him back; and he cried out to the man of God who came from Judah, saying, "Thus says the LORD: 'Because you have disobeyed the word of the LORD, and have not kept the commandment which the LORD your God commanded you, but you came back, ate bread, and drank water in the place of which the LORD said to you, "Eat no bread and drink no water," your corpse shall not come to the tomb of your fathers.'" So it was, after he had eaten bread and after he had drunk, that he saddled the donkey for him, the prophet whom he had brought back. So when he was gone, a lion met him on the road and killed him. (1 Kings 13:20–24)

God certainly did use a man with major character flaws to reprove one of His saints, and there is no reason to believe that He would not do this today.

"But didn't you explain earlier that we should first take the beam out of our own eye before we attempt to remove the speck from our brother's eye?"

I did. But that instruction is given to the reprover, not to the reprovee. You may not use character flaws in your reprover's (parent's) life as an excuse for despising, rejecting, or hating reproof.

2. Thinking that if your reprover has a poor attitude when he reproves you, you don't have to listen.

Do you remember the account of Shimei, who cursed King David?

> Now when King David came to Bahurim, there was a man from the family of the house of Saul, whose name was Shimei the son of Gera, coming from there. He came out, cursing continuously as he came. And he threw stones at David and at all the servants of King David. And all the people and all the mighty men were on his right hand and on his left. Also Shimei said thus when he cursed: "Come out! Come out! You bloodthirsty man, you

rogue! The LORD has brought upon you all the blood of the house of Saul, in whose place you have reigned; and the LORD has delivered the kingdom into the hand of Absalom your son. So now you are caught in your own evil, because you are a bloodthirsty man!" (2 Sam. 16:5–8)

David took this foul-mouthed, disrespectful insult seriously; one of his men even offered to do away with this scoundrel.

Then Abishai the son of Zeruiah said to the king, "Why should this dead dog curse my lord the king? Please, let me go over and take off his head!" (2 Sam. 16:9)

In fact, not only did David take Shimei seriously, he actually saw the rebuke as coming directly from God Himself.

And the king said, "What have I to do with you, you sons of Zeruiah? So let him curse, because the LORD has said to him, 'Curse David.' Who then shall say, 'Why have you done so?' " And David said to Abishai and all his servants, "See how my son who came from my own body seeks my life. How much more now may this Benjamite? Let him alone, and let him curse; for so the LORD has ordered him. It may be that the LORD will look on my affliction, and that the LORD will repay me with good for his cursing this day." And as David and his men went along the road, Shimei went along the hillside opposite him and cursed as he went, threw stones at him and kicked up dust. (2 Sam. 16:10–13)

You must learn to look beyond the reprover's poor attitude to determine from Scripture whether the reproof is legitimate. This is not to say that you cannot convict your reprover for his poor attitude after examining his reproof in light of Scripture. The basic issue, however, is that God may be sovereignly using the rebuke (poor attitude notwithstanding) to drive you back to His Word. With Bible in hand (or in mind), you must prayerfully consider the legitimacy of each admonition.[3]

3. And, if the reproof is from a parent, even though you may not see a biblical basis for it, you may still be obligated to change your (nonsinful) behavior in deference to them (see Eph. 6:1).

3. Viewing the reproof as too small a concern.

Some of the most intense parent/teen conflicts occur over the most seemingly inconsequential matters.

God is concerned with how we handle the little things: "He who is faithful in what is least is faithful also in much; and he who is unjust in what is least is unjust also in much" (Luke 16:10). Therefore, you should consider not the smallness of the offense but its sinfulness. If what you are being reproved for is a transgression of God's law, then regardless of how small, the reproof is valid. You cannot rightly overlook it on the basis of insignificance.

4. Failing to focus on the attitude lying behind the words and actions to which your reprover is reacting.

When certain Samaritans did not welcome our Lord with open arms, James and John responded with vengeance: "Lord, do You want us to command fire to come down from heaven and consume them, just as Elijah did?" (Luke 9:54).

His rebuke cut right through the inappropriateness of their words, as well as through the hastiness of their proposed action, by focusing on the heart of the issue: their vengeful attitude. "You do not know what manner of spirit you are of" (i.e., "You don't have a clue as to how terrible your attitude is!"; v. 55).

When a wise teen is reproved for things he has said or done, he will examine his life and look beyond the surface problem to determine whether there are underlying habit patterns or attitudes that ought to be replaced with biblical ones. Sadly, this concept is practiced perhaps least often in the home, whether between husband and wife or between parent and child.

Our minds frequently work like a computer, constantly storing information and classifying it in categories. When a certain number of unpleasant or painful actions are inflicted upon us by a particular member of our family, a buzzer goes off and our computer displays the file of offenses and the category they fall into (e.g., "specific ways my mother has falsely accused me over the years"). There, the updated offense pops up in full color on the screen of our minds: "#121: Accusing me of purposely forgetting my book bag at school so that I wouldn't be able to do my homework." The Bible forbids us to keep lists such as these, even in our minds, for 1 Corinthians 13:5 states that love "doesn't keep records of wrongs" (CCNT).

The knowledge that this dynamic is all too "common to man" (1 Cor. 10:13) should motivate us to look for those categories of sinful attitudes that may have triggered such a display in the mind of our reprover—especially if that reprover is a parent who lives with us and knows us better than most others. See if you can identify the underlying attitudes behind the following sets of reproofs (i.e., if you can tell what is at the top of each of these computer screens).

A. Computer screen number one:
   1. Leaving your socks on the floor at night before going to bed
   2. Not cleaning out the sink (or bathtub) after shaving in the morning
   3. Leaving your empty glasses at various places around the house

B. Computer screen number two:
   1. Exaggerating about the quality of your schoolwork
   2. Not volunteering essential information about certain unlawful activities of your friends
   3. Hiding contraband in your room

C. Computer screen number three:
   1. Spending more money than you had budgeted for a particular nonessential item
   2. Eating much more food than is necessary for maintaining life
   3. Gossiping about the pastor's daughter

The underlying attitude in the first set of reproofs is *inconsiderateness*. The teenager in the second set has a problem with *dishonesty*. The heading at the top of the third set of behaviors is *lack of self-discipline*. By learning to "read between the lines" in this manner, you will be better prepared to respond to your reprover and may save yourself from having to face similar reproofs in the future.

5. Justifying (excusing) your behavior.

Perhaps one of my most important tasks as a biblical counselor is to identify and correct the many excuses that counselees offer to justify their irresponsible (unbiblical) behavior. Here are a few of the most common ones, accompanied by a typically remedial comeback:

Counselee: "I can't."

Counselor: "You can't say 'can't' as a Christian. The Bible says that you can do all things through Him who strengthens you. Please don't say, 'I can't'; say 'I will' or 'I won't.' "

Counselee: "You can't teach an old dog new tricks."

Counselor: "That may be true of dogs, but you are not a dog. You are a Christian, and God says that you can change at any age. You therefore must change any behavior that is inconsistent with the character of the Lord Jesus Christ."

Counselee: "If I told my parents the truth, it would hurt them too much."

Counselor: "Telling your parents the truth may very well hurt them, but not nearly as much as if they caught you telling a lie. Telling the truth may hurt for a while, but telling a lie will hurt longer and more intensely. That is one reason why God forbids you to do it."

Counselee: "You can't expect me to do that, because I didn't have a role model growing up."

Counselor: "You may not have had a role model as you were growing up, but now that you are a believer, you have *the* role model: the Lord Jesus. God expects you to learn how to do that because He has commanded you to do it. God has not asked you to do anything without first promising (in Phil. 2:13) to provide you with the wisdom, the ability, and even the desire to do it."

Counselee: "I know that I should have done my counseling homework, but I was so busy this week I just didn't have time to do it."

Counselor (opening the file drawer of his desk and reaching in as if to grasp a handful of something): "I don't have any whiffle dust to sprinkle on you to change you instantly. God doesn't work that way. God changes your behavior from the inside out as you work on your own salvation with fear and trembling. Change is hard for you and for me, but there is something harder than changing, and that is not changing! The way of the transgressor is hard. The choice is yours: hard work for a while or a hard way for life. Which will it be?"

6. Resorting to one of the following instinctive acts of revenge:

- Pouting (allowing your hurt feelings to prevent you from responding properly)
- Giving your reprover "the silent treatment"
- Reminding your reprover that he is not perfect either
- Blame-shifting (blaming your reprover for provoking you into a sinful response)
- Threatening (blackmailing your reprover into "dropping the charges" by means of fear and intimidation)
- Throwing a temper tantrum

Next let's consider some righteous responses to reproof.

Turning at Reproof: "If you turn at my reproof, behold, I will pour out my spirit to you; I will make my words known to you" (Prov. 1:23 ESV—*turning* in the Old Testament means repenting).
Hearing Reproof: "The ear that listens to life-giving reproof will dwell among the wise" (Prov. 15:31 ESV—*hearing* means responding God's way).
Heeding Reproof: "Poverty and disgrace come to him who ignores instruction, but whoever heeds reproof is honored" (Prov. 13:18 ESV).

1. Thank God.

Your first response should be to acknowledge that you are aware of His sovereignty by giving thanks to Him. "In everything give thanks; for this is the will of God in Christ Jesus for you" (1 Thess. 5:18). Have an attitude like David's: "Let the righteous strike me; it shall be a kindness. And let him reprove me; it shall be as excellent oil; let my head not refuse it" (Ps. 141:5).

2. Ask yourself, "What is my reprover really saying to me?"

This is the biblical alternative to sinful response number four above: "Reproof is more effective for a wise man than a hundred blows on a fool" (Prov. 17:10). Looking for the truth in what your reprover is saying, whether it involves your wrong attitude or your God-dishonoring habit pattern, is a practical way to put on humility. Unless you are absolutely certain that your reprover is mistaken, it's best to leave the "door ajar" for the possibility that your sinful heart has blinded you from seeing the truth.

3. Thank your reprover for his reproof.

This step not only will communicate your receptivity to the reproof, but also will prepare your brother for more open communication. Keep in mind that when a wise man is reproved, he responds in love: "Rebuke a wise man, and he will love you" (Prov. 9:8). Remember also that an appropriate response on your part enhances the radiance of your character: "Like an earring of gold and an ornament of fine gold is a wise reprover to an obedient ear" (Prov. 25:12).

4. Ask yourself, "What message might God be trying to get through to me?"

If your focus is on the attitude of the one who reproves you, you may miss any truth that is apparent in the reproof. If you prayerfully look beyond the bad attitude of your reprover and ask God to show you from Scripture whether or not the reproof is valid, you may walk away with new insight into how you can become more Christlike. One of the strongest verses in the whole Bible concerning God's sovereignty addresses itself to the fact that no one can say that anything comes about without God allowing it to happen: "Who is he who speaks and it comes to pass, when the Lord has not commanded it?" (Lam. 3:37)

5. If the reproof is legitimate, take steps to correct the problem.

At this point, your responsibility is to implement whatever scriptural solutions are necessary to bring about biblical change. Having heard the Word, you must become a "doer of the Word" (see

James 1:22). As we have seen, a biblical solution usually involves replacing (putting off) the sinful behavior with (putting on) the biblical alternative to that behavior. In other words, it will not be enough for you simply to stop practicing the wrong you have done. You must also make it your goal (through the enabling of the Holy Spirit) to practice the right you had not done, so that doing right becomes second nature (see Eph. 4:22–24) for you.

6. If you are convinced from Scripture that you have not sinned as per the reproof, wait until your reprover knows that you have spent some time thinking it through; then, in a timely fashion, consider explaining your viewpoint to him.

The apostle Paul had a rather lengthy answer to the Corinthians, who were aware of an accusation that some had made toward him: "My defense to those who examine me is this . . ." (1 Cor. 9:3).

If you come to the conclusion that you have not sinned, it may be appropriate to communicate this conclusion to your reprover. But again, if the reprover is one of your parents, you may still be obligated to change your behavior, even though the behavior for which you were reproved is not a sin.

Now that you have some guiding principles for receiving reproof, what will you do with them? Could it be that by virtue of reading this appendix, you have been reproved for not following these precepts in your dealings with others (especially Mom and Dad)? If so, you must not act like the proverbial fool whose chief characteristic is not to listen to instruction. Rather, you must change your habitual miscommunication skills by practicing these biblical communication skills so that you will be able to speak them fluently.

Appendix C

PARENTAL PROVOCATION WORKSHEET

YOU CAN LEARN HOW TO respond biblically to the sinful things your parents do to provoke you. No matter what others do to you, you have a responsibility to respond as a Christian. Put a check in the box next to each thing your parents *regularly* do to provoke you to anger. Under each provocation that you checked, identify your *typical* responses (what you usually say to yourself, what you usually say or do to them, and what you are most often longing for that their provocation prevented you from having). When you have finished, go back and biblically evaluate your responses. For each one that is unbiblical, try to identify at least two God-honoring alternatives to choose from the next time you are provoked.

Mom Dad

☐   ☐   When my folks lack marital harmony
         I think to myself . . .
         I respond to them by . . .
         I want . . .

☐   ☐   When my folks maintain a child-centered home
         I think to myself . . .
         I respond to them by . . .
         I want . . .

☐ ☐ When my folks model sinful anger
I think to myself . . .
I respond to them by . . .
I want . . .

☐ ☐ When my folks consistently discipline in anger
I think to myself . . .
I respond to them by . . .
I want . . .

☐ ☐ When my folks scold
I think to myself . . .
I respond to them by . . .
I want . . .

☐ ☐ When my folks are inconsistent in discipline
I think to myself . . .
I respond to them by . . .
I want . . .

☐ ☐ When my folks have double standards
I think to myself . . .
I respond to them by . . .
I want . . .

☐ ☐ When my folks are legalistic
I think to myself . . .
I respond to them by . . .
I want . . .

☐ ☐ When my folks do not admit when they are wrong
I think to myself . . .
I respond to them by . . .
I want . . .

☐ ☐ When my folks continuously find fault with me
I think to myself . . .
I respond to them by . . .
I want . . .

☐ ☐ When my folks reverse God-given roles
I think to myself . . .
I respond to them by . . .
I want . . .

☐ ☐ When my folks do not listen to my opinion (or my side of the story)
I think to myself . . .
I respond to them by . . .
I want . . .

☐ ☐ When my folks compare me unfavorably with others
I think to myself . . .
I respond to them by . . .
I want . . .

☐ ☐ When my folks do not have time to talk with me
I think to myself . . .
I respond to them by . . .
I want . . .

☐ ☐ When my folks do not praise me
I think to myself . . .
I respond to them by . . .
I want . . .

☐ ☐ When my folks fail to keep promises to me
I think to myself . . .
I respond to them by . . .
I want . . .

☐ ☐ When my folks give me too much freedom
I think to myself . . .
I respond to them by . . .
I want . . .

☐ ☐ When my folks do not give me enough freedom
I think to myself . . .
I respond to them by . . .
I want . . .

☐ ☐ When my folks make fun of me
I think to myself . . .
I respond to them by . . .
I want . . .

☐ ☐ When my folks call me names
I think to myself . . .

I respond to them by . . .
I want . . .

☐ ☐ When my folks have unrealistic expectations for me
I think to myself . . .
I respond to them by . . .
I want . . .

☐ ☐ When my folks show favoritism to my siblings
I think to myself . . .
I respond to them by . . .
I want . . .

☐ ☐ When my folks . . .
I think to myself . . .
I respond to them by . . .
I want . . .

☐ ☐ When my folks . . .
I think to myself . . .
I respond to them by . . .
I want . . .

☐ ☐ When my folks . . .
I think to myself . . .
I respond to them by . . .
I want . . .

☐ ☐ When my folks . . .
I think to myself . . .
I respond to them by . . .
I want . . .

Appendix D

IDOLATROUS "LOVES" IN THE BIBLE

THINGS THAT PROCEED OUT OF THE HEART
MARK 7:20–23

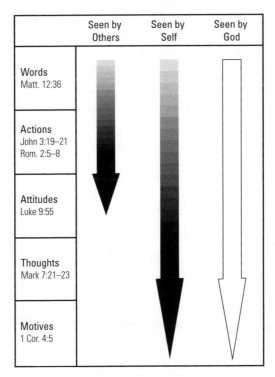

	Seen by Others	Seen by Self	Seen by God
Words Matt. 12:36			
Actions John 3:19–21 Rom. 2:5–8			
Attitudes Luke 9:55			
Thoughts Mark 7:21–23			
Motives 1 Cor. 4:5			

#	Idolatrous "Loves" in the Bible	Scripture Reference
1.	*Love of money* For the love of money is a root of all sorts of evil, and some by longing for it have wandered away from the faith, and pierced themselves with many a pang.	1 Timothy 6:10
2.	*Love of self* But realize this, that in the last days difficult times will come. For men will be lovers of self.	2 Timothy 3:1–2
3.	*Love of approval* For they loved the approval of men rather than the approval of God.	John 12:43
4.	*Love of control (power)* I wrote something to the church; but Diotrephes, who loves to be first among them, does not accept what we say. For this reason, if I come, I will call attention to his deeds which he does, unjustly accusing us with wicked words; and not satisfied with this, neither does he himself receive the brethren, and he forbids those who desire to do so, and puts them out of the church.	3 John 9–10
5.	*Love of pleasure* But realize this, that in the last days difficult times will come. For men will be lovers of self, lovers of money, . . . lovers of pleasure rather than lovers of God.	2 Timothy 3:1–2, 4
6.	*Love of food* He who loves pleasure will become a poor man; he who loves wine and oil will not become rich.	Proverbs 21:17
7.	*Love of sleep* Do not love sleep, lest you become poor.	Proverbs 20:13

8.	*Love of darkness* And this is the judgment, that the light is come into the world, and men loved the darkness rather than the light; for their deeds were evil.	John 3:19
9.	*Love of simplicity* How long, O naive ones, will you love simplicity? And scoffers delight themselves in scoffing, and fools hate knowledge?	Proverbs 1:22
10.	*Love of cursing* He also loved cursing, so it came to him; and he did not delight in blessing, so it was far from him.	Psalm 109:17
11.	*Love of evil and falsehood* You love evil more than good, falsehood more than speaking what is right. Selah.	Psalm 52:3
12.	*Love of silver and abundance* He who loves money will not be satisfied with money, nor he who loves abundance with its income.	Ecclesiastes 5:10
13.	*Love of one's own life* He who loves his life loses it; and he who hates his life in this world shall keep it to life eternal.	John 12:25
14.	*Love of this present world* For Demas, having loved this present world . . .	2 Timothy 4:10
15.	*Love of the things in the world* Do not love the world, nor the things in the world. If anyone loves the world, the love of the Father is not in him.	1 John 2:15

Appendix E

COMMON WAYS IN WHICH TEENAGERS SIN AGAINST THEIR PARENTS[1]

THE FOLLOWING CHECKLIST will help you to identify some of the ways in which you have sinned against your mother and father. Although not exhaustive, this list represents some of the more common areas of sinful behavior and neglect among Christian teenagers. The wording is already in the second person ("you"), rather than the third person ("Mom" or "Dad"), to facilitate the confessing of your sins directly to both of your parents later on. As you prayerfully read over each item, put a check next to those offenses that you believe are applicable to you. Fill in any blank spaces with more precise information. Confess each transgression to God and then prepare your heart to confess them, when appropriate, to each parent individually.

Remember, the more specific you can be, the more your parents will realize the degree to which you are serious about changing and the extent to which you are cognizant of how your sins have hurt them. This should make it easier for them to truly forgive you. Also, the more specifically you can identify your bad habits, the easier it will be for you, by God's grace, to change. Don't forget to add to the list any additional offenses

1. The material in this appendix has been adapted and expanded from Wayne A. Mack, *Homework Manual for Biblical Living, vol. 2: Family and Marital Problems* (Phillipsburg, NJ: P&R Publishing, 1980), 35-38. Used by permission.

that are not mentioned on it specifically. When you are finished, look back over the checked items for specific patterns of behavior (common denominators) that may indicate a particular life-dominating sin (such as selfishness, anger, irresponsibility, lack of self-control, and so on).

Mom Dad

☐ ☐ I have not been a good example of a Christian.

☐ ☐ I don't have a consistent personal devotional life (Bible reading, prayer).

☐ ☐ I'm inconsistent with church attendance.

☐ ☐ I'm not as involved in Christian ministry as I should be.

☐ ☐ I've been bitter and resentful toward you.

☐ ☐ I don't reveal my heart to you as much as I should, especially in the area of_____.

☐ ☐ I've consistently disobeyed you.

☐ ☐ I've been disrespectful to you.

☐ ☐ I've stolen _____from you.

☐ ☐ I've been inconsiderate of your

_____.

☐ ☐ I don't ask for your advice or opinion as often as I should.

☐ ☐ I don't show enough respect for your wishes.

☐ ☐ I don't give you enough assistance with

_____.

☐ ☐ I've taken you for granted by

_____.

☐ ☐ I've not truly forgiven you for

_____.

☐ ☐ I've been lazy in _____.

☐ ☐ I expect you too often to drop what you're doing and give me attention.

☐ ☐ I have unreasonable expectations of you, such as

_____.

☐ ☐ I don't keep my _____ neat and orderly.

☐ ☐ I don't express myself clearly and thoroughly.

☐ ☐ I interrupt you when you are talking.

☐ ☐ I often let my attention wander when you're talking to me.

☐ ☐ I'm often too preoccupied with

_____.

☐ ☐ I'm impatient with you, especially when

_____.

☐ ☐ I raise my voice rather than responding to you softly and graciously.

☐ ☐ I use biting sarcasm when I talk to you.

☐ ☐ I respond to you before I understand what you are really saying.

☐ ☐ I judge your thoughts and motives without knowing them.

☐ ☐ I don't cover in love (or overlook) many things you do that irritate me.

☐ ☐ I don't put the best possible interpretation on things you do, but tend to be critical and even suspicious of you at times.

☐ ☐ I use manipulation and intimidation to get my own way.

☐ ☐ I say and do things that are vindictive in nature.

☐ ☐ I don't show you enough respect, especially by

_____

☐ ☐ I spend too much time away from home.

☐ ☐ I make important decisions without your counsel.

☐ ☐ I leave food, clothing, and other apparel lying around the house.

☐ ☐ I selfishly play music too loudly.

☐ ☐ I murmur and complain about _____.

☐ ☐ I make excuses for my _____.

☐ ☐   I blame others for my mistakes.

☐ ☐   I'm too critical of you.

☐ ☐   I'm not as thankful as I should be for all of God's mercy and blessings.

☐ ☐   I'm selfish when it comes to offering you help but often expect you to help me whenever I need it.

☐ ☐   I seldom express my appreciation for you or compliment you.

☐ ☐   I'm too concerned about what others think of me.

☐ ☐   I spend too much money on _____.

☐ ☐   I'm too stingy with my _____.

☐ ☐   I've said unkind things to you.

☐ ☐   I've said unkind things about you.

☐ ☐   I have not been totally truthful with you about _____.

☐ ☐   I use profanity.

☐ ☐   I call you names.

☐ ☐   I drink alcohol.

☐ ☐   I smoke cigarettes.

☐ ☐   I watch too much television.

☐ ☐   I make excuses or simply refuse when you ask me to do certain things that you want me to do, such as _____.

☐ ☐   I have bad manners, especially when it comes to _____.

☐ ☐   I have blamed you for my mistakes, such as _____.

☐ ☐   I don't ask for help when I have a serious problem.

☐ ☐   I don't often admit when I'm wrong.

☐ ☐   I'm too distrustful of you, especially when it comes to _____.

☐ ☐   I make promises to you and do not follow through with them.

☐ ☐   I don't give enough of my _____ to the church.

☐ ☐ I lose my temper or _____ when you don't give me what I want.

☐ ☐ I get my feelings hurt too easily (I'm too sensitive because of my pride).

☐ ☐ I haven't worked hard enough at correcting my annoying habits, especially _____ and _____.

☐ ☐ I sometimes resist or resent your helpful suggestions.

☐ ☐ I don't run errands gladly.

☐ ☐ I'm too selfish with my _____.

ADDITIONAL AREAS OF FAILURE:

☐

☐

☐

☐

☐

Appendix F

PARENTAL EVALUATION FORM

1. Name:
2. For the week of

    This form has been designed to help you evaluate the progress your teen is making in the specific areas listed below. Please identify (on lines A–C below) three areas in which you would like to see him or her improve. At the end of the week, assess any improvement in your teen's behavior according to the rating scale. Don't forget to include under "Specifics" any additional comments you believe would be beneficial. The Parental Evaluation Form is intended to be used in conjunction with some form of additional accountability (on the part of a parent, counselor, youth leader, or pastor). Please discuss with your teen who you believe would be best suited to help hold him or her accountable.

SCALE:

1. Things got worse
2. No improvement
3. Little improvement
4. Some improvement
5. Considerable improvement

Circle the appropriate number and give specific instances. Additional comments may be included on the back. Thank you for your sincere evaluation.

A. _____

I   2   3   4   5

Specifics:

B. _____

I   2   3   4   5

Specifics:

C. _____

I 2 3 4 5

Specifics:

Appendix G

EXTRA JOURNALS

THE REMAINING PAGES of this book contain additional copies of the Anger Journal and the Heart Journal. These are provided for you to fill out directly in this book or to photocopy and use when and where necessary.

ANGER JOURNAL

1. What happened that provoked me to anger? (What were the circumstances that led to my becoming angry?)

_____

_____

_____

_____

_____

_____

_____

2. What did I say and/or do when I became angry? (How did I respond to the circumstances?)

_____

_____

_____

_____

_____

_____

_____

3. What does the Bible say about what I said and/or did when I became angry? (What is the biblical terminology for what I said and/or did when I became angry?)

   _____

   _____

   _____

   _____

   _____

   _____

   _____

4. What should I have said and/or done when I became angry? (How could I have responded biblically when I became angry?)

   _____

   _____

   _____

   _____

   _____

   _____

   _____

HEART JOURNAL

1. What happened that provoked me to anger? (What were the circumstances that led to my becoming angry?)

_____

_____

_____

_____

_____

_____

_____

_____

2. What did I say to myself (in my heart) when I became angry? (What did I want, desire, or long for when I became angry?)

_____

_____

_____

_____

_____

_____

_____

_____

3. What does the Bible say about what I said to myself when I became angry? (What does the Bible say about what I wanted when I became angry?)

_____

_____

_____

_____

_____

_____

_____

_____

4. What should I have said to myself when I became angry? (What should I have wanted more than my own selfish/idolatrous desires?)

_____

_____

_____

_____

_____

_____

_____

_____